It Happened
in the
Cimarron
Country

Other Books by Stephen Zimmer:

People of the Cimarron Country
Philmont: An Illustrated History (with Larry Walker)
Vision, Grace and Generosity (with Nancy Klein)
For Good or Bad: Stories of the Cimarron Country
Philmont: A Brief History of the New Mexico Scout Ranch (with Larry Walker)
Western Animal Heroes: An Anthology of Stories by Ernest Thompson Seton
Cowboy Days: Stories of the New Mexico Range
Vermejo Park Ranch: A History
Express UU Bar Ranch: A History
Parker's Colt: A Novel of New Mexico Ranch Life

It Happened

in the

Cimarron
Country

Stephen Zimmer
and Steve Lewis

A Double Z Bar Ranch Book

For our dear wives

and our children.

It Happened in the Cimarron Country
Copyright © 2013 by Stephen Zimmer *&* Steve Lewis

All images are from the authors' collections, unless otherwise noted. Design, editing, and production: Steve Lewis

Library of Congress Control Number: 2013940137

ISBN: 978-0-9851876-7-5 (softcover)
    978-0-9851876-8-2 (hardcover)
    978-0-9851876-9-9 (eBook)

ZZ To contact the authors:
    Double Z Bar Ranch
    230 Rayado Creek Road
    Cimarron, New Mexico 87714

 Published by Eagle Trail Press
    PO Box 3671
    Parker, Colorado 80134
    info@EagleTrailPress.com

Acknowledgements

Over the years people have invested lifetimes researching, recording, and preserving the events of the past. Their labors must have seemed insignificant at times, but those of us living today owe them a great debt of gratitude. As we look into our history we are better able to understand the changes that have taken place, how our society came to be the way it is, and how we might steer it toward a brighter future. The book you now hold in your hands could not have been written apart from the efforts of those who have gone before us.

We are especially indebted to scholars and writers such as William Keleher, Jim Berry Pearson, and Lawrence Murphy who tirelessly investigated early events in the Cimarron country. Along with others interested in northern New Mexico, they laid the foundation for historical research upon which more recent writers like David Caffey and others are building.

Historical preservation takes many forms, and Cimarron's own Gene Lamm has spearheaded the effort to capture and archive hundreds of old photographic images taken in the Cimarron country. A picture really is worth a thousand words, and Gene's work will have an impact for generations.

Special thanks go to David T. Kirkpatrick whose career as a field archaeologist began as a grad student when he directed the archaeology program at Philmont Scout Ranch in the early 1970s. Since that time he has conducted archaeological studies and excavations throughout New Mexico. The results of his work have been published in several scholarly journals, and we are privileged to include in this volume his recent survey of the prehistoric cultures of the Cimarron country.

Thanks to Thayla Wright at Arthur Johnson Memorial Library, Roger Sanchez at Raton Museum, Coi Drummond-Gehrig at Denver Public Library Western History Collection, Daniel Kosharek at Palace of the Governors Photo Archives, Sarah Gilmor at History Colorado Center, David Werhane and Robin Taylor at Philmont Scout Ranch, Gene Lamm at Old Mill Museum, Beni Jo Fulton at Elizabethtown Museum, Chuck Speed at Dawson Association, Warren Lail, Bruce and Brenda Black, Quentin Robinson, and Larry McLaughlin for providing materials from their collections.

SAZ & SRL

Contents

Introduction

This book is a labor of love. There is something magnetic about the Cimarron country that has always attracted a special breed of people, forming a strong bond deep in the soul. Once you have been captured by this amazing place, you are never the same again.

Steve Zimmer's previous book focused on the *People of the Cimarron Country*, telling the stories of more than two dozen hardy residents who made homes for themselves and others in this rugged land. Now this companion volume focuses on some of the important places and events that have occurred in the Cimarron country. There are many unique spots on this landscape which treasure up secrets and have seen incredible things. The short vignettes included here recount some special events from across the area, and they are placed in the book more-or-less chronologically.

Beginning with the earliest known inhabitants, archaeologist David Kirkpatrick shares some of his (and others') discoveries about the lives of ancient peoples who traveled and lived in the Cimarron country for literally thousands of years. David is truly a "history detective" who has dedicated his life to piecing together evidence that helps us understand what happened before records were kept and photographs were taken.

More recently, other native peoples claimed the Cimarron country as their home. There are many fascinating tales about the places they lived and the events that shaped their relationship to newcomers in the area. Those newcomers included the Spanish colonists who spread northward from the Rio Grande Valley, as well as the rugged breed of

1

trappers and traders who roamed the countryside in search of adventure and economic opportunity.

The Santa Fe Trail, the first commercial highway in the West, brought with it new people, exciting times, and a fresh awareness of the potential of this beautiful land. Through the years there has been a virtual parade of individuals across the Cimarron country, from Spanish conquerors to Mexican land grant holders and American traders, soldiers, settlers, and ranchers.

Conflict has sometimes erupted, as it did during the many Indian battles, the Mexican War for Independence, the Mexican-American War, the Colfax County land grant dispute, and many smaller skirmishes over property and water rights—all of which were life-changing for those directly involved in them.

The Cimarron country has it all: Indian, mountain man, and pioneer legends. Cowboy and ranching tales. Stagecoach and early railroad adventures. Gold fever! Heroes and villains. Hangings and outlaws. Corporate greed. Overwhelming individual generosity and philanthropy. Dramatic births and tragic deaths. Struggles and triumphs. Beginnings and endings.

You've probably heard the old saying: "I wasn't born here, but I got here as fast as I could." That is certainly true for both of the Steves who authored this book. Steve Zimmer grew up in the ranching country of west Texas, so he was born and bred to the southwest. By the time he was ready for college he had tasted the Cimarron country. It was love at first sight and he never left. Steve Lewis was raised on the outskirts of Kansas City where the Santa Fe Trail began, and as a young boy he was fascinated by its tales. In his late teens he traveled to see where the trail led, and the Cimarron country worked its way into his life. Even though he later roamed far and wide, this land has always held a special place in his heart. The same can be said for countless others who have experienced the magnetic attraction of the Cimarron country.

Steve Zimmer and Steve Lewis first met forty years ago as staff members in remote mountain camps at Philmont Scout Ranch. Zimmer shared his many stories about prehistoric peoples, native tribes, and pioneering ranchers with the Boy Scouts who visited his backcountry camps. Lewis portrayed the lively mountain men and gold miners at "living history" sites, where Scouts could experience firsthand what life would have been like in those early days. Their great bond of friendship and their mutual love of the Cimarron country brought them back

1870s photo of Cimarron, New Mexico, looking south toward the Tooth of Time.
Courtesy of Old Mill Museum.

together in their "grayer" years to collaborate on this book. The history of the Cimarron country contains a treasure trove of heroic examples and valuable lessons for all of us to learn, and this book shares many of them for today's interested readers.

What about you? Do you have your own connection to the Cimarron country that motivated you to pick up this book? If not, we would encourage you to take the plunge. Share these stories with us, then travel to the Cimarron country to see the stark beauty and feel for yourself the magnetic pull of its mountains, valleys, and plains. We promise you will never be the same and will be enriched beyond measure for the experience.

Timeline of the Cimarron Country

1100—Ponil Canyon becomes home to ancient people groups.

1525—Jicarilla Apache people migrate into Cimarron country.

1610—Spanish establish Santa Fe as capital of northern provinces.

1706—Spanish Ulibarri expedition visits Cimarron area.

1807—Zebulon Pike expedition escorted to Santa Fe.

1810—Beginning of Mexican War of Independence from Spain.

1821—Mexico wins independence from Spain.

Commercial use of Santa Fe Trail by William Becknell.

1833—Santa Fe trade increases; Bent, St. Vrain, and Company builds Bent's Fort on Arkansas River.

1841—Charles Beaubien and Guadalupe Miranda receive land grant.

1846—Mexican War and American occupation of New Mexico.

1848—Lucien Maxwell colonizes Rayado.

1857—Maxwell moves ranch to Cimarron River.

1858—Maxwell acquires Miranda's share of grant.

1860—US Congress confirms Beaubien and Miranda Land Grant.

1861—Maxwell erects Aztec grist mill.

Apache/Ute Indian agency at Maxwell's ranch.

US mail route changed to use Raton Pass via Cimarron.

1864—Beaubien dies; Maxwell and wife inherit his share of grant.

1865—Wootton builds toll road over Raton Pass.

1866—Gold discovered along Willow Creek in Moreno Valley.

1867—Gold discovered on Ute Creek below Baldy Mountain.

1868—Road opened through Cimarron Canyon to Moreno Valley.

Kit Carson dies at Fort Lyon, Colorado.

1869—John Dawson buys 3,700 acres from Lucien Maxwell.

1870—Manly Chase buys 1,000 acres from Lucien Maxwell.

Maxwell sells land grant to British investors.

Maxwell Land Grant & Railway Company established.

1871—Charles Kennedy hanged in Elizabethtown.

1873—Beginning of CS Ranch.

1875—Maxwell dies at Fort Sumner.

Reverend F.J. Tolby assassinated in Cimarron Canyon.

1879—Santa Fe Railroad enters New Mexico over Raton Pass.

1880—Maxwell Cattle Company established by MLGCo.

1887—US Supreme Court confirms 1,714,764 acre Maxwell grant.

1893—M.M. Chase wins World's Fair gold medal for apples.

1898—Wilson buys land from MLGCo; establishes WS Ranch.
1899—Shoot out at Black Jack's hideout in Turkey Canyon.
1901—Black Jack Ketchum hanged in Clayton, New Mexico.
   W.H. Bartlett buys Vermejo Park from MLGCo.
   Dawson sells ranch to Dawson Fuel Company.
   J.C. Osgood buys Colorado portion of Maxwell Land Grant.
1905—St. Louis, Rocky Mountain & Pacific Company established.
1906—Phelps Dodge Corporation buys coal mines at Dawson.
   SLRM&P railroad reaches Cimarron.
1907—Continental Tie & Lumber Company organized in Cimarron.
   Cimarron & Northwestern Railway builds into Ponil Canyon.
1910—George Webster, Jr., buys Urraca Ranch; plants vast orchard.
1920—Eagle Nest Dam completed.
1922—Waite Phillips purchases Urraca Ranch.
1927—Phillips family moves into new Villa Philmonte mansion.
1930—Ponil Canyon logging ceases and C&N tracks removed.
1938—Waite Phillips donates 35,857 acres to Boy Scouts of America.
1941—Waite Phillips donates 91,538 acres to Boy Scouts of America.
1942—SLRM&P Railroad abandoned.
   Philmont Scout Ranch established.
   McDaniels family buys remainder of Phillips' ranch.
1945—W.J. Gourley buys WS Ranch.
1948—Gourley buys Vermejo Park.
1950—Dawson mines closed and town abandoned.
1963—Baldy country added to Philmont Scout Ranch.
1973—Pennzoil buys Vermejo Park.
1982—Pennzoil donates Valle Vidal to Carson National Forest.
1996—Ted Turner buys Vermejo Park Ranch.
2006—Bob Funk purchases UU Bar Ranch.

The Legend of Lovers' Leap

Standing outlined against the sky and on the edge of the precipice stood a man and maiden. The man was dressed as a chief. They were talking earnestly, and although not a sound broke the stillness of the night, it was evident that he was pleading with the girl. Now the man is on bended knee pleading with her, but with a gesture of disdain, she turns and steps a few paces away. As she does, the man rises and totters on the edge of the rock and hurls himself off shouting in a loud voice, *"Asi se murio su novio"* (so your lover dies).

Some of us hurried to where the man's body lay, while others went to the top of the rock where the maiden yet stood as if carved of stone.

The man we found to be Chirina, son of the chief of the Cochiteños tribe. The maiden—she was a beautiful paleface who was found on the plains after a band of settlers had been attacked by Apaches. She had grown among the tribe, and it had been the dream of Chirina's life to make her his squaw.

Tenderly guiding Enriqueta, for that was her name, back to the camp and burying the body of her lover at the base of the rock, we broke camp and started

for Taos. When we arrived the maid was taken to Faustino and given into the care of Miceala, his squaw. After weeks of lingering illness, she died. Remiglo, our medicine man, said it was from a broken heart, although she would never speak of the scene enacted on that summer night.

Carefully, we bore her frail body, wrapped in a beautiful blanket, back to the base of the rock at the opening to Urraca Park and digging another grave, laid her in it beside her lover. From that day we have always known that rock as "Lovers' Leap."

Originally appeared in the *Denver Republican*, reprinted in the *Raton Range*, September 18, 1902.

Prehistoric Peoples of the Cimarron Country

R ising above the western edge of the Great Plains, the Park Plateau was the home of prehistoric Native Americans for over 1,000 years. This area, known as the Cimarron District to New Mexico archaeologists, is a piñon and juniper woodland with grassy meadows. Several canyons, including the North and Middle Poñil, have creeks flowing through lush bottom lands that eventually empty into the Cimarron River. These woodlands, canyons, and nearby plains provided the wild plants and animals used for food and clothing by the prehistoric Native Americans. The earliest occupants were the Paleoindian big game hunters, followed by the Archaic hunters and gathers, and finally the Ancestral Puebloan farmers.

Paleoindian Hunters (9500 BC - 5500 BC)

Arriving by way of the Bering Land Bridge, the Paleoindians were the first humans in the New World and were in the Southwest by 9500 BC. The Paleoindians hunted numerous now-extinct species of very large mammals or mega-fauna. These mammals included the woolly mammoth, mastodon, bison, camel, horse, and sloth that lived at the end of the Pleistocene era when the climate was much cooler and wetter. The Paleoindian culture is divided into several time periods based on diagnostic projectile points which have been discovered. Archaeologists refer to some of these hunters as the Folsom Culture (9000 BC - 8000 BC) because the first of their archaeological sites was found near

By David T. Kirkpatrick, PhD, RPA.

the village of Folsom, New Mexico, located northeast of Cimarron. Folsom points have a characteristic channel or depression running the length of both sides of the point. In 1908 George McJunkin, a black cowboy, was riding the pasture on the Crowfoot Ranch when he observed a deeply buried bed of bison bones eroding out of Wild Horse Arroyo. Several years later McJunkin dug in the bone bed and found a Folsom point which he sent to the Denver Museum of Natural History in 1918.

Excavations by archaeologists and paleontologists from the Denver Museum of Natural History yielded large fluted projectile points in association with the bones of *bison antiquus*. Jesse Higgins continued these excavations between 1926 and 1928, finding more projectile points with the bones.

Folsom point, with distinctive groove
along the entire length.
Courtesy of David Kirkpatrick.

Leading American archaeologists were invited to see the *in situ* relationship between the fluted points and the bones, and by 1928 the archaeologists agreed that prehistoric man had indeed hunted extinct Pleistocene animals. This was a landmark event in American archaeology for it established that the Native Americans had lived in North America for over 10,000 years.

While Paleoindian sites have not been found in the Cimarron area, isolated projectile points from the period have been located. The nearest discovery was just east of Cimarron in Van Bremmer Canyon. On the plains, these points have been found in the Canadian River canyon, Bueyeros, and in the central Rio Grande Valley near Albuquerque, west of the Sangre de Cristo Mountains.

The Paleoindians traveled in a seasonal cycle, following bison herds and hunting other game animals with the *atlatl*, a spear thrower. They usually collected seasonally available plants, nuts, and berries for food. Unless they were busy processing game at a kill site, such as at Wild Horse Arroyo, they probably only stayed a few days in any one location. In other parts of New Mexico, these rare sites have sparse scatters of flakes from the manufacture of projectile points, scrapers, and chipped stone tools.

Their seasonal movement helps to explain why their sites are so hard to find. As the climate changed to warmer and drier conditions, the larger Pleistocene mammals that were important to the Paleoindian diet became extinct. The Paleoindian peoples had to adapt to changing conditions by hunting smaller game such as deer, antelope, rabbits, hares, and rodents, as well as using more of the native plants for food and medicine.

Archaic Hunters and Gatherers (6000 BC - AD 200)

The Archaic peoples were descendants of the Folsom culture, and they were also seasonal hunters and gatherers who were highly mobile across the plains. Archaic sites have been found in the rock shelters of the Canadian River canyon southeast of Cimarron, along the front of the Park Plateau between Cimarron and Raton, and in the uplands of the Poñil and Vermejo River canyons north of Cimarron. Sites have been discovered on flat terraces at varying elevations above the canyon floors. Often the sites are located near the terrace edges so the occupants would have an excellent view of the canyon bottom lands where deer and other animals would come to graze and drink from the streams.

These open campsites have dense scatters of flakes from making large projectile points and bi-facial tools, including scrapers and choppers. These tools were important during the processing of animals for food, and they were used in preparing hides for clothing, bags, and other uses. The projectile points from the Cimarron area are often large corner-notched points commonly made of horn-fels, a very hard fine-grained rock. These points would have been attached to the foreshaft of the atlatl spear. Hammer stones and cores for making tools are often found with the scattered flakes.

The Archaic peoples were nomadic, traveling across relatively large areas to hunt and gather seasonally available plant foods. In the spring, creek bottoms would have been the source for new growth greens and late spring grass seeds. In the summer, the seeds of lamb's quarters and

Archaic atlatl dart.
Courtesy of Warren Lail.

9

pigweed were mature, as was the fruit of the banana yucca. Piñon pine nuts, chokecherries, squawbush fruit, and sunflower seeds were among numerous shrubs that were eagerly collected. Their fall harvest of plant foods, plus hunting deer, rabbits, hares, and other small game animals, was important because these were the stores of food that the Archaic peoples depended on to survive the cold and snowy winter months.

In addition to chipped stone tools, the Archaic peoples created stones that they shaped by grinding, such as *manos* and *metates* for crushing seeds, berries, and nuts that were collected seasonally. Manos were created using oval river cobbles which easily fit in a woman's hand. Metates were often flat slabs of sandstone, quartzite, or other coarse-textured rock, with a slight depression which provided a grinding surface for the seeds. The cooking process for plants and meat included stone boiling, where hot rocks were placed in a hanging hide bag or sealed basket that contained a stew or soup. As the rocks cooled, they were removed to the fire and were exchanged for new hot rocks. The remains of these cooking hearths and scatters of fire-cracked rock are still visible at many of these sites.

In some rare instances, archaeologists have also found dwellings in shallow rock caves where a family could be sheltered from the wind and rain. Some of these shelters contain stratified deposits with the remains of baskets, sandals, and other perishable artifacts. The artifacts from these sites are important because they add to our understanding

Prehistoric cliff shelter, taken from the opposite side of Box Canyon.
Courtesy of Warren Lail.

of how the Archaic peoples adapted to their environment between the canyon lands of the Park Plateau and the level lands on the western Great Plains.

One of the most important adaptations of the Late Archaic period was the shift from gathering seasonal wild plants to growing domesticated crops like corn, beans, and squash. Growing these plants in the summer months would have provided a more reliable food surplus for the winter months, rather than relying solely on harvests of piñon pine nuts, berries, and seeds for food. This shift to an agricultural or horticultural pattern probably took several hundred years. Hunting deer and small game continued to be important for supplementing their diet with meat during this transition.

Ancestral Puebloan Agriculturalists (AD 200 - 1300)

The Ancestral Puebloans lived in the Cimarron region for about 1,100 years. The earliest archaeological sites, dating to the Vermejo Phase (AD 200 - AD 700), consist of scattered flakes and the remains of a circular rock-walled structure that probably housed a single family. The rooms are about 15 feet in diameter, usually with a clear area surrounded by collapsed rock walls. The walls were made by stacking sandstone slabs to a height of about three feet. The upper wall and roof would have been made from piñon and juniper branches which were then covered with mud. Pieces of dried mud have been found with impressions of branches and even corn cobs, and this provides evidence for the composition of the upper walls and roof.

These sites are located on elevated landforms such as low elevation terraces or high elevation cliff edges along the streams. Their diet was a mix of native animal and plant foods, like the Archaic peoples, with the addition of corn and beans. Their fields were probably at the mouths of small side canyons opening onto the larger valley floor. The plants would have been watered with summer rain runoff, or in dry years water may have been carried in hide bags from the nearby streams. There is no evidence of structures for storing the corn and bean crops. Weedy plants such as lamb's quarters, pigweed, and sunflowers would have been harvested from the fields and other open areas. Pine nuts, juniper berries, chokecherry seeds, and prickly pear fruits were important plant foods in their diet.

Their stone tool collection included smaller projectile points for bows and arrows rather than the larger points used earlier on atlatl spears. This provides evidence of a major change in their hunting strategies. Their projectile points were small and corner-notched, made from hornfels, chalcedony, obsidian, and other fine-grained minerals. They also created bi-facial stone tools for cutting and chopping, as well as quartzite hammer stones and cores for making these tools and points. Quartzite and sandstone manos and metates for grinding corn have also been found. Pottery bowls and jars were not found during this phase.

Pedregoso Phase (AD 700 - 900)

Around AD 700 there was another change in the settlement pattern from the terraces and cliff edges to the valley floor. The Pedregoso Phase is characterized by an abundance of fire-cracked rocks that were used to cook corn in underground bell-shaped ovens. A first known site in the North Poñil Canyon is located at the upper edge of the valley floor. The only known architectural feature is a possible ramada based on a series of postholes.

Bell-shaped pits were used to cook and store corn, beans, and other foods. The ones used for cooking have baked and reddened walls from fires built to heat rocks inside the oven. When the fire died down, ears of corn in the husk would have been placed inside the hot oven. A large sandstone slab was placed over the 18 to 24 inch opening, and then the edges were sealed with mud. The cooking process probably took several hours or even overnight. Storage pits are the same shape but lack the hard baked edges. When the storage pits and ovens were no longer used, they were filled with trash, which consisted of charcoal, fire-cracked rocks, animal bones, and flakes from stone tools. In some cases these pits served as graves, usually closed with a large slab.

Fire pit discovered in North Ponil Canyon.
Courtesy of Philmont Scout Ranch.

The collection of chipped and ground stone artifacts is similar to those in the Vermejo Phase. A few potsherds of coarse-tempered and low-fired brownware were found at this site. These sherds may represent the introduction of pottery making in the Cimarron area. The use of pottery to cook foods over flames or coals is a major improvement over the earlier stone-and-bag boiling technique. Corn and beans require a cooking time and temperature that cannot be achieved with stone boiling.

The Pedregoso Phase represents a major change in the lifestyle of the Ancestral Puebloans. They began to shift from a nomadic life of following the seasonal cycles to a more sedentary existence. Crops continued to be planted at the mouths of side canyons, with additional fields on the valley floor. More time would have been needed to water the plants and to protect the crops from rabbits, hares, and other small rodents which were used for food when captured. The excavation and maintenance of the bell-shaped ovens and storage pits, some of which are 6 feet in diameter and 4 feet deep, would have involved spending more time in one place. With larger harvests, the pits would have been used for storing corn and beans during the winter months.

Escritores Phase (AD 900 - 1100)

With their increasing reliance on agriculture, the Ancestral Puebloans became more sedentary. The Escritores Phase is characterized by deep, circular pit houses with roof entrances. The houses had a central fire hearth, and the smoke exited through the opening in the roof. Fresh air came in through an exterior ventilator shaft on the southeast side of the structure. The pit houses were dug into the ground to a depth of three or four feet. The roof was supported by a square four-post beam and viga superstructure which was covered with smaller logs, branches, and plants and then plastered with mud and dirt. This type of structure would have provided a tight shelter for the cold winter months.

Living activities took place on the roof as well as inside the pit house, and specific work areas have been identified inside. Chipped stone tools were manufactured in an isolated area so as to not scatter sharp flakes around the floor. There were also small storage pits in the floor of these structures.

The collection of artifacts resembles that of the Pedregoso Phase but without the abundance of fire-cracked rock. Storage containers may have been built outside in above ground structures. The major artifact addition during the Escritores Phase consists of pottery bowls and jars for serving, cooking, and storage. The most common ceramic vessels were plain grayware jars and decorated black-on-white bowls and jars. The discovered ceramics include Kiatuthlanna Black-on-White, Red Mesa Black-on-White, and Kana'a Neck-Banded pottery, which indicate that trade relations had been established with Ancestral Puebloans living in the Rio Grande Valley to the west of Cimarron.

With an increasing population, more of the valley floor was probably being planted with crops. Native plant foods and wild animals, however, were still important to supplement the corn, bean, and squash in their diet.

Poñil Phase (AD 1100 - 1200)

A major change in architecture occurred around AD 1100. An increase in population led to a shift in the housing pattern, with more people living in above-ground pueblos in the lower portion of Poñil Canyon. The valley floor of lower Poñil Canyon is much broader than the upstream areas of Middle and North Poñil Canyons. With a larger population, more cultivated fields would have been required to grow the crops of corn, beans, and squash needed to feed families during the winter months. Wild game animals and plants remained an important part of their subsistence activities.

Poñil Phase sites range from a single pueblo to a group of pueblos that probably formed a small community. In North Poñil Canyon, a small pueblo has been excavated which consists of one large room with two smaller rooms behind the living area. The pueblo rooms are outlined by vertical slabs. Based on the absence of rock rubble, the walls were probably made of coursed adobe layers, with the vertical slabs serving as stabilizing structures.

Coursed adobe construction involves stacking layers of mud on top of previously dried mud layers to gain the desired height. As the walls deteriorated over time, melting away through erosion, an archaeologist would find a mound of earth which encapsulated the old rooms. Posts have been discovered in the interior areas which would have supported a wood and dirt-covered roof. Metates and other artifacts on the roof also indicate to archaeologists that some daily activities

Ponil points.

David Kirkpatrick at an early dig in North Ponil Canyon.
Courtesy of Philmont Scout Ranch.

took place on top of the dwelling. The entry door was probably in the center of the roof, and like the pit houses, it also served as a smoke hole for the hearth located in the middle of the room.

Many of the small rock shelters and overhangs along the North and Middle Poñil canyons were also occupied for varying periods of time. These sites often consist of several stratified levels, indicating repeated occupation over the years. In addition to stone tools, archaeologists have found perishable artifacts such as sandals, basketry, mats, and wooden items.

In the lower Poñil Canyon, the Chase Orchard Pueblo is a community of eleven mounds, though not all of these pueblos may have been occupied at the same time. Excavations have uncovered pueblo rooms built over older rooms, indicating reuse of the same location over time. A possible kiva was discovered, which would have been a room for holding religious ceremonies. The floor area of these pueblos is greater than that of the pit houses from the previous period. This suggests that the family living in these rooms was an extended family consisting of several generations, instead of a single nuclear family with parents and their own children.

The artifact collections from these sites includes both side- and corner-notched arrow points, hammer stones, cores, grooved mauls and axes, drills, and arrow shaft straighteners. The collection also includes ground stone tools, including trough-shaped metates with both one-hand and two-hand manos. Metates were also found with vertical walls that keep the corn kernels from moving off the metate when being ground. The collection of ceramics included bowls, notably Taos

Black-on-White, as well as undecorated jars classified as Taos Gray, Taos Punctate, and Taos Incised, along with an unknown gray corrugated ware. It is not known if these vessels were made locally or were traded from pueblos in the Taos area, west of Cimarron in the upper Rio Grande Valley.

Bone artifacts recovered from excavated Poñil Phase sites include awls, scrapers, and bone beads. The bone beads, also found in the Pedregoso and Escritores phase sites, were often made from the long bones of birds and rabbits. Shell beads have also been recovered, which also indicates trading with the Ancestral Puebloan peoples west of the Sangre de Cristo Mountains.

Cimarron Phase (AD 1200 - 1300)

During the Cimarron Phase, the population was living primarily in pueblos along lower Poñil Creek and the Cimarron River above the confluence of the streams. These two areas had a high population density with numerous sites, each containing several house mounds. The pueblos were of different sizes and shapes. Some had a single square

Scouts assisting with an active archeological dig in Ponil Canyon.
Courtesy of Philmont Scout Ranch.

room, while others consisted of a linear row of small rectangular rooms. Others had a rectangular room block with square-shaped rooms, or a main square block with rooms along the exterior walls. Some of these sites appear to have been occupied during the Poñil Phase and possibly earlier as well. A few Cimarron Phase pueblos were occupied in the upper North and Middle Poñil canyons.

Agriculture continued to be the main source of plant foods. Although it is difficult to determine, it is likely that fields were watered by small diversion ditches from the Cimarron River and Poñil Creek. The crops consisted of corn, beans, and squash. Natural plants like sunflowers, lamb's quarters, and pigweed were probably encouraged and harvested for greens and seeds. Hunting small rodents, rabbits, deer and possibly antelope would have continued to be important.

The stone and ceramic artifacts resemble those of the Poñil Phase. There was a shift from smaller corner-notch projectile points to larger side-notched points. Their collection of ceramics included a new type of grayware called Cimarron Plain. The vessels were decorated with incised, punctuate, and neck-banded styles. This pottery was probably manufactured at the Cimarron pueblos. Jars were frequently found, but Cimarron grayware bowls are quite rare. These jars would have been used for both cooking and storage. Potsherds from Santa Fe Black-on-White bowls were also discovered at these sites. Santa Fe Black-on-White is common at the Ancestral Puebloan sites in the northern Rio Grande valley, and it was made only in the bowl form. This indicates that the Cimarron people were probably trading in the Taos area for these decorated bowls, which would have been used as serving vessels.

The End of an Era

Sometime around AD 1300 the Ancestral Puebloans abandoned the Cimarron area. Why they left remains an unsolved mystery. One factor might have been a change in the climate, with several years of drought that may have caused crop failures. There is no evidence of warfare with other groups who were migrating into the area. These families probably moved to live near their relatives and trading partners in the northern Rio Grande Valley. Whatever the reason, it is clear that these people have left a fascinating record of their existence which has shaped the face of the Cimarron country to this very day.

About the Author

Dr. David T. Kirkpatrick is a Registered Professional Archaeologist and Associate Director of Research for *Human Systems Research*, a non-profit archaeology firm in Las Cruces, New Mexico. He is past president of the New Mexico Archaeological Council and a member of the Archaeological Society of New Mexico. Over the last forty years he has conducted surveys and excavations on sites associated with Paleo-Indian, Archaic, Ancestral Puebloan, and Mogollon cultures, as well as studies of historic ranching, mining, railroad, and military sites. He began his career while a graduate student at Washington State University when he fell in love with the Cimarron country and directed the archaeology program at Philmont Scout Ranch in the early 1970s.

Warriors of the
Mountains and Plains

When Spanish conquistador Don Francisco de Coronado explored the upper Rio Grande in 1540 he learned from the indigenous Pueblo Indians that they had been attacked some fifteen years before by unknown raiders who lived on the vast plains to the east of their towns. These raiders primarily subsisted by hunting buffalo, but they coveted the corn, beans, squash, and other vegetables grown by the horticultural Pueblos.

After Don Juan de Oñate and his colonists established the first Spanish settlement on the Rio Grande in 1598, they also had contact with the raiding Indians from the plains. Scholars today recognize the raiders as Apache Indians who spoke the Athabascan language. They had entered the southern Plains in the early 16th century after a long migration from their ancestral homeland in northern Canada. They were separated into several groups that the Spaniards knew as Jicarillas, Cuartelejos, Sierra Blancas, and Faraons.

By the early 18th century Jicarilla bands had settled in the foothills and canyons of the Sangre de Cristo Mountains in what is now north-eastern New Mexico, forced there by their enemies, Utes and Comanches, who commanded the buffalo plains to the east. The Spaniards referred to the location as La Jicarilla. The tribal appellation is derived from an Aztec Indian word, *jicara*, which the Spanish used to refer to receptacles such as baskets, pots, or drinking cups. Presumably they applied this word to the Jicarilla bands because they made pots and

---

By Stephen Zimmer

19

Jicarilla Apache horsemen entering their village, circa 1870s.
Courtesy of Library of Congress Photographs Division.

baskets with which to cook and store their food.

Although the Jicarillas were driven into the area, it was advantageous for them because they could grow crops in the canyon bottoms that emerged from the east side of the mountains. They had learned to farm from contact with the Pueblo Indians on the Rio Grande. Aside from hunting in the mountains they also ventured onto the plains to hunt buffalo, but they had to be vigilant in order to avoid attacks from their numerically superior enemies.

The Jicarillas developed friendly relations with the Spaniards, not only because of the trading opportunities but also because they offered protection from their enemies. Two Spanish expeditions were sent into the Jicarillas' country in the early part of the 18th century. The first was led by Captain Juan de Ulibarri in 1706 in an effort to subdue the Comanches and protect the friendly Jicarillas. Another expedition, this time led by the governor of the province, Don Antonio de Valverde, followed Ulibarri's footsteps in the summer of 1719. Both expeditions failed to encounter the Comanches, and the Jicarillas were left to fight their enemies on their own.

By the mid-18th century many of the Jicarillas moved their camps west over the mountains to the Taos Valley and the upper Rio Grande in order to avoid their enemies from the plains. The Spaniards called them Olleros or mountain valley people. Eight extended family groups remained on the east side of the Sangre de Cristos in present-day

Teepees in a Jicarilla Apache village, circa 1870s.
Courtesy of Library of Congress Photographs Division.

Colfax, Mora, and San Miguel counties. The Spaniards referred to these Jicarillas as Llaneros or plains people. The Cimarron Valley was their favorite stronghold along with sites near present-day Mora, Ocate, Ute Park, and along the Ponil and Vermejo Rivers.

The Jicarillas also wove baskets and made micaceous pottery with which to process, store, and cook food. In addition to hunting buffalo on the plains, they hunted deer, elk, antelope, rabbits, and turkeys and gathered berries, nuts, and roots in the mountains. They either lived in pit houses, teepees, or flat roofed dwellings that were supported by upright posts.

In the middle of the 18th century the Utes and Comanches broke relations, and the Utes allied with their former enemies, the Jicarillas. These two tribes developed a strong relationship that included intermarriage and continued into the 19th century.

When American traders began crossing Jicarilla land over the Santa Fe Trail in the 1820s, the Jicarillas periodically attacked their freight trains in search of plunder and scalps. In the spring of 1848 when mountain man Lucien Maxwell established a ranch on the Rayado River in the middle of Jicarilla territory, the Indians resented the intrusion and repeatedly raided the settlement.

In June of that year they attacked a pack train owned by Maxwell as it travelled through the Raton Mountains, and they drove off the outfit's mules and horses. The next year the Jicarillas attacked the wagon

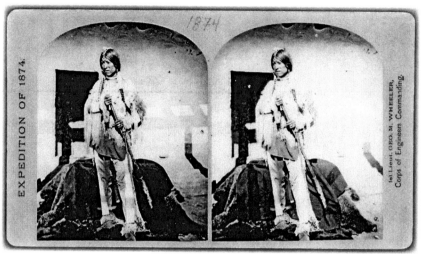

*Shee-zah-nan-tan, a Jicarilla Apache brave in traditional costume,
taken in northern New Mexico, 1874.*

Courtesy of Library of Congress Photographs Division.

train of J.M. White near Point of Rocks east of Rayado, killing White
and the other traders and capturing his wife and young child. Dragoons guided by Kit Carson eventually located the raiders, but they
were not in time to save Mrs. White and her child.

Because of winter cold and snow, the Jicarillas did not bother the
Rayado settlement or any Santa Fe trains until the spring of 1849. In
order to secure his settlement, Maxwell convinced the United States
Army to station dragoons at the ranch to protect it as well as passing
Santa Fe Trail travelers. Ten mounted dragoons arrived from Taos in
the spring under the command of Sergeant William C. Holbrook. Unfortunately, their presence did not fully deter the Jicarillas who raided
the ranch and made off with most of the ranch's riding stock in April.
As a result, two companies of dragoons under Major William Grier
were added to the forces at Rayado.

In June the Jicarillas again raided Rayado and drove off another
herd of Maxwell's livestock, killing an Army bugler and an employee
at the ranch in the process. That raid precipitated an Army expedition
against the Apaches in July which saw few casualties, but resulted in the
recapture of a great number of cattle, sheep, horses, and mules that had
been stolen from Rayado.

In an effort to stop the Jicarilla raids the Indian agent for New Mexico, James Calhoun, convinced the Indians to come to the territorial
capital and negotiate a peace treaty. After lengthy council sessions the

two sides agreed that the Jicarillas would confine themselves to certain "specified territorial limits, cultivate the soil, cease their depredations, and relinquish all captives and stolen property." In exchange the Indians were to receive annual subsistence rations, farm implements, and other considerations.

Most of the Jicarillas complied with the provisions of the treaty, with the exception of the Llaneros on the east of the Sangre de Cristos who continued to bristle because of American encroachment on their land. In addition a few dissident Olleros committed raids in the Taos area over the next few years, which culminated in a pitched battle against the US Army near Embudo Mountain south of Taos in March of 1854. During the confrontation twenty-two dragoons under the command of Lieutenant John W. Davidson were killed and thirty-six were wounded.

As a result of that battle, the army declared all out war on the Jicarillas and unrelentingly pursued several bands of them for the next four months. No significant confrontations occurred because the Indians had better knowledge of the country and were successful in evading the military forces. Another expedition sent against the Jicarillas the following year had no better results.

By the end of the summer of 1855, however, the Jicarillas had grown weary of the constant harassment by military forces and the necessity of continually attempting to evade confrontation with them. As a result several of their leaders sent peace offerings to Territorial Governor David Meriwether. The two sides met in Abiquiu in August and after a short deliberation entered into a treaty whereby the Jicarillas again agreed to confine their camps and settlements to certain prescribed areas and to stop their raiding in return for annual rations.

The Jicarillas were attached to the Ute Agency in Taos with Kit Carson as the agent. Most of the Llaneros maintained their old camps on the east side of the Sangre de Cristos. Periodically their young warriors raided white settlements in the area or attacked Santa Fe traders in violation of the treaty, but by and large the Indians kept to themselves and followed their

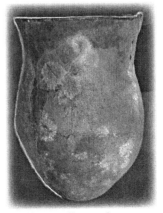

Early Jicarilla Apache pottery.
Courtesy of David Kirkpatrick.

Jicarilla brave and squaw in traditional costume, taken in northern New Mexico, 1874.
Courtesy of Library of Congress Photographs Division.

old patterns of farming in the summer and hunting on the plains or in the mountains in the fall.

At the beginning of the Civil War, Kit Carson resigned his position as agent and joined the 1st New Mexico Volunteers which had been organized to protect the Territory against a Confederate invasion from Texas. The Government decided to move all of the 1,500 Jicarillas and their agency over the mountains to Maxwell's Ranch at Cimarron in order to keep them out of harm's way.

William F.M. Arny was appointed as their first agent. A reformer and ex-preacher, Arny developed plans to improve conditions for the Indians and to make them more self sufficient, primarily by establishing schools and providing them with clothing, better food rations, and farm tools. He leased 1,280 acres from Maxwell in Ponil Canyon north of Cimarron for $20 per year. Maxwell also agreed to supply the Indians with beef rations, as well as wheat and corn ground from his grist mill, albeit at inflated prices.

School rooms, offices, a council room, and an agent's house were erected on agency grounds. Arny wrote his supervisors that he "erected at my own cost a corral for horses and cattle, and intended this fall to fence about five acres of ground adjoining the agency for cultivation as a vegetable garden for the use of the agency; also I have ploughed twenty acres more, which I intended to plant next spring in wheat, corn, and vegetables, and divide the small patches, to be tended by

Ration tokens discovered at Jicarilla Apache Indian agency site in Ponil Canyon.
Courtesy of David Kirkpatrick.

such Indians as were willing to work, the produce to belong to the Indian who cultivated the patch, and thus I hoped to be able to gradually induce the Indians of this agency to quit roaming over the country and cultivate industrial habits."

Nonetheless, the Jicarillas' age-old habits proved difficult to change. They continued to roam the mountains in search of game that was increasingly hard to find. Consequently, the Indians faced near starvation at times, especially when government ration funding fell short.

The Jicarillas were able to exact retribution of sorts against their plains enemies in November of 1864 when Colonel Kit Carson, commanding the 1st New Mexico Volunteers, came to Maxwell's ranch and recruited 75 Jicarillas and Utes as scouts for a planned expedition against the Kiowas and Comanches. The tribesmen were promised spoils of horses, captured weapons, and food stuffs in return for their involvement.

Carson and his Indians joined the US forces at Ft. Bascom on the Canadian River and marched eastward to find the hostiles. When the hostile villages were discovered, Carson ordered an attack that was initially successful. Several hours into the battle, however, he recognized that he had engaged the west end of a large encampment that continued down the river for ten miles. When increasing numbers of enemy warriors entered the battle from the downstream villages, Carson wisely chose to withdraw, save his command, and return

Jicarilla Apache girl in feast dress.
Courtesy of Library of Congress Photographs.

to New Mexico. For their part, the Jicarillas were given a number of captured horses. Because they failed to take any scalps during the battle they were forced to trade for one in order to conduct a scalp dance on the journey home.

At their agency many of the Jicarillas succumbed to drinking alcohol that was illegally provided to them by unscrupulous traders. To make matters worse, they often bartered their government rations for the watered down whiskey. While in a drunken state some of the Indians harassed residents and employees of Maxwell's ranch which created much ill will.

Conditions at the agency had deteriorated so much that in the summer of 1866 General James H. Carleton, District Commander of New Mexico, travelled to Cimarron to investigate. He wrote in his report,

> I find that the Utes and Apaches who reside near this place are wholly destitute of food, their game is entirely gone, and they are forced to kill the stock of the people or starve. Their killing of the people's cattle and sheep herds leads to collisions; already blood has been spilled and there is much hostile and bitter feeling on the part of the Indians. In this matter the Indians cannot be blamed. The Indian department does not feed them and there is really left but one alternative for the Indians, that is to kill stock or perish. We cannot make war upon people driven to such extremities. We have taken possession of their country. Their game is all gone and now to kill them for committing depredations solely to save life cannot be justified. This is not only a true story, but the whole story.

Lucien Maxwell proposed a solution to the problem by offering his land grant for sale to the United States government as a reservation for the Indians. Included in the offer was a tract of land forty by sixty miles in area, his grist mill, and the ranch buildings. The Indian Department declined the offer, however, since rich gold deposits were discovered in the Moreno Valley on the west side of the grant.

The Jicarillas were incensed over the influx of so many miners into their territory. Fortunately, there were few altercations between the Indians and the gold seekers, and the Indians felt relieved when the gold strikes began to play out after a few years and many miners began to leave the fields.

The Jicarilla situation was further complicated when Lucien Maxwell chose to sell the land grant to British investors in 1869. Maxwell's decision saddened the Indians because they trusted him as a friend and appreciated how he helped to feed them in time of need. The British company developed plans to permanently remove the Jicarillas from the grant, and they were successful in doing so in September 1876. The Indians were forced to move their camps south to the Sacramento Mountains on the reservation of their linguistic relatives, the Mescalero Apaches.

In his landmark history of the Cimarron country, Larry Murphy cogently summarized Jicarilla treatment by the United States during the Cimarron agency period.

> No aspect of the history of the Cimarron country is more dismal than the US's handling of the Ute and Apache. Pushed out of their traditional homeland by farmers, ranchers, and miners, the Indians were unable to feed themselves. The government seldom provided adequate food or supplies. Well-meaning but inept agents, as well as corrupt and self-seeking agents, did little to alleviate the suffering. Frequently the Army prevented Indians from stealing or killing,

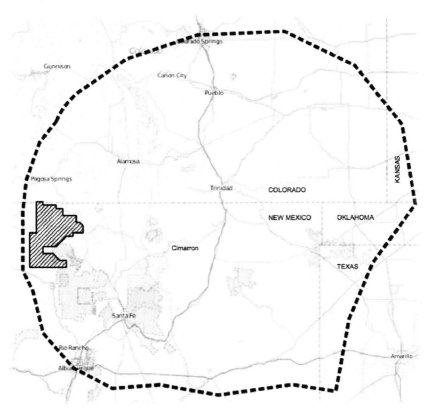

Traditional Jicarilla Apache range (outline),
with approximate reservation area shown at left.

but soldiers did little to solve long-term problems. Only the final removal of the tribesmen brought peace and opened the area to more development.

The Jicarillas were never content living with the Mescaleros and they longed to return to their homeland. They explained to their agent that "the Great Spirit had created them in the Cimarron area, where they had lived for as long as anyone could remember. The bones of their forefathers had been buried there. The climate was pleasant and the water healthful...where the government had promised they could remain forever."

Finally in an 1887 executive order, President Grover Cleveland assigned lands to the Jicarillas to serve as a reservation. Located west of the Rio Grande in the far western part of their historic range, the land at the time was deemed marginal as far as potential white settlement was concerned. Although some miles distant from the Cimarron country, the Jicarillas rejoiced in having a permanent home.

Their struggles have not been easy, but the tribe has made a remarkable transition. Today the tribe is among the most prosperous in the United States because of the wise development of their mineral, timber, and grazing resources on the reservation. The Jicarilla Apache Nation is a federally recognized tribal entity, and in 1937 they organized a formal government, adopted a constitution, and elected traditional leaders to their first official tribal council.

Their reservation is located in the San Juan Basin, which is rich in fossil fuel resources. This basin is one of the largest producers of oil along the Rocky Mountains and the second largest producer of natural gas in the United States. The Oil and Gas Administration of the Jicarilla Apache Nation manages nearly 2,200 producing oil and gas wells on the Jicarilla reservation. They promote the development of mineral resources while protecting the beauty of their ancestral lands.

Over the years they have gone from a semi-nomadic existence to having a designated homeland which is now supported by the oil and gas, forestry, ranching, casino gaming, and tourism industries on the reservation. Through it all they have not forgotten their native traditions, and the Jicarilla continue to be known for their pottery, basketry, and bead work.

The First Roundup

On a clear day in September 1599, sixty Spanish soldiers rode forth from their headquarters on the Rio Grande. The sun glistened off their armor as they crossed the river and headed east, destined for the high plains of the Llano Estacado. Don Juan de Oñate, the leader of the newly established Spanish colony in New Mexico, had ordered the expedition to find buffalo. After locating the "native cattle," as the Spaniards referred to them, the soldiers were to gather a herd and drive it back to the colony. Oñate hoped that a breeding herd of the wild animals could be established to serve as food for the settlers.

The Spaniards only knew about buffalo from information supplied by the local Indians, and up to that time most of them had never actually seen a buffalo. But from what they had learned, they were satisfied that the wild animals could be handled much like their own domestic cattle. After spending a short time on the plains, however, they quickly understood that buffalo were much wilder than any bovine they had ever seen.

Sketch of a buffalo drawn by a member of the Oñate expedition.

The expedition, under the command of Sergeant

From "The First Roundup" by Stephen Zimmer, *Western Horseman*, March 2002: 134-140.

Early sketch of a vast buffalo herd spread across the plains as far as the eye can see.

Major Vincente de Zaldivar, was well equipped with supplies and "many droves of mares" for packing and riding. The soldiers first traveled east to the Pecos River and then proceeded to the foot of the mountains where they met a group of Indians who furnished them with a guide to find the buffalo.

After a few more days of traveling across the plains of eastern New Mexico, the expedition climbed on top of the caprock and for the first time saw buffalo watering at a playa lake. The next day they came upon a herd estimated at a thousand head. Zaldivar decided to build a large corral to pen as many as possible. Unfortunately the herd moved to the east before the soldiers finished the corral, so they abandoned it and followed the tracks of the herd.

In a few days the soldiers reached a spot south of the Canadian River where they discovered evidence of a large herd that had recently been driven off by Indians. A day later the Spaniards encountered another group of Indians and decided to camp near them. During the next few days, Zaldivar made several observations about how the Indians lived.

He was notably impressed by the serviceability of their tents "made of tanned hides, very bright red and white in color and bell-shaped, with flaps and openings, and built as skillfully as those of Italy." He further noted that "the tanning is so fine that, although it should rain bucketfuls, it will not pass through nor stiffen the hide, but rather upon drying it remains as soft and pliable as before." Even though the tents were large, able to accommodate "four different mattresses," he commented that they did not weigh more than fifty pounds.

Zaldivar was amused at how the natives transported their belongings using "medium-sized shaggy dogs" as pack animals. The Indians had great numbers of them. In his account of the expedition he reported that "it is a sight worth seeing and very laughable to see them traveling...nearly all of them snarling in their encounters, traveling one after another on their journey. In order to load them, the Indian women seize their heads between their knees, and thus load them or adjust the load, which is seldom required because they travel along at a steady gait as if they had been trained by means of reins."

The Spaniards continued their march after a few days, and soon found another large buffalo herd. Several members of the expedition estimated that it contained more cattle than could be found on "three of the largest ranches in new Spain." As a result, Zaldivar again ordered his men to build a corral, which they completed in three days. It was constructed of cottonwood logs, and was so large that the Spaniards believed it would hold 10,000 head.

When the corral was finished, the soldiers made plans to pen the buffalo. They were still under the assumption that the animals would be easy to pen, primarily because they seemed nearly tame, given how closely they wandered past the camp. Furthermore, the Spaniards were convinced that buffalo were poor runners because of their ungainly appearance. However, in the next several days they would learn firsthand how intractable those "native cattle" could be.

The Spaniards' first attempt at driving buffalo started out well enough, although it soon went awry. The soldiers got behind a big bunch and slowly headed them toward the wings of the corral. But as the buffalo neared the wings, the leaders of the herd turned back and stampeded toward the surprised soldiers. The expedition's chronicler, Juan Bocanegra, described the occasion by saying, "It was impossible to stop them because they are terribly obstinate cattle, courageous beyond exaggeration, and so cunning that if pursued they run, and if their pursuers stop or

Spanish soldier horseback on the Great Plains.

Buffalo herd stampeding across the prairie, pursued by horsemen.
Courtesy of Library of Congress Photographs Division.

slacken their speed, they stop and roll, just like mules, and with this respite renew their run."

In the following days the Spaniards made several more attempts to pen the buffalo, but all were equally unsuccessful. They discovered to their dismay that buffalo were not as docile as they first appeared. Bocanegra described them as being "remarkably savage and ferocious, so much so that they killed three of our horses and badly wounded forty" others. He wrote that the buffalo attack from the side with their sharp horns "so that whatever they seize they tear very badly."

Having failed at driving the buffalo into the corral, Zaldivar decided on a new strategy. He ordered his men to bring in calves because he recognized the futility of trying to rope adults. Unfortunately, even though his soldiers caught many calves, none of them survived the stress of being drug or even carried on a horse.

Thoroughly frustrated, Zaldivar finally turned the expedition back to the Rio Grande and reported to Oñate the results of his unsuccessful mission. From his experience on the plains, he suggested that the only way buffalo could ever be driven to the colony would be to crossbreed them with Spanish bulls in hopes that the calves could be gentled enough to drive. Unfortunately, history provides no record that this experiment was ever carried out.

Santa Fe Trail Through Cimarron

For half a century before the coming of the railroad, the Santa Fe Trail exerted an important influence on the growth and development of the Cimarron country. As on the trail itself, there are many twists and turns in the story of this famous road through the wilderness. The destination was the city of Santa Fe, which had been established in 1610 by its Spanish conquerors as the capital of the northern province of *Nuevo México*. From there the "Royal Road of the Interior Land"—*Camino Real de Tierra Adentro*—led south through Chihuahua and Durango to Mexico City, and ultimately to Vera Cruz which was the nearest port on the Gulf of Mexico. That coastal city was almost 2,000 miles from Santa Fe, and the journey was an arduous one for merchants supplying the needs of the northern provinces.

Before 1800 almost all of the land west of the Mississippi River was claimed by Spain. France had controlled the Louisiana Territory until 1762, when it gave this land to its Spanish ally. In 1800, however, France took back the Louisiana Territory under an agreement negotiated by Napoleon Bonaparte. Because of a pressing need for funds, Napoleon then sold the Louisiana Territory in 1803 to the United States for around $15,000,000.

Several US government expeditions were dispatched to learn as much as possible about this new land. In 1806 Lieutenant Zebulon Pike led twenty men to explore the Arkansas River and if possible to find the headwaters of the Red River, which formed one of the southern

---

By Steve Lewis

boundaries of Louisiana Territory. Pike ended up on the Rio Grande instead of the Red River, however, and this was within Spanish jurisdiction. Soldiers from Santa Fe arrested Pike and eventually escorted him to Chihuahua for questioning. After his release Pike published an account of the expedition, and by 1810 his book became so popular that it was read throughout America and Europe. In his report Pike commented on the trade and commerce of northern New Mexico. He even recorded specific details about prices for goods in Santa Fe.

> The following articles sell in this province, which will show the cheapness of provisions and the extreme dearness of imported goods: Flour sells, per hundred, at $2; salt, per mule-load, $5; sheep, each, $1; beeves, each, $5; wine, per barrel, $15; horses, each, $11; mules, each, $30; superfine cloths, per yard, $25; fine cloths, per yard, $20; linen, per yard, $4, and all other dry goods in proportion. The journey with loaded mules from Santa Fe to Mexico, and returning to Santa Fe, takes five months.

Pike also mentioned that he found an American in Santa Fe he identified as James Pursley, who arrived in 1805 and "has been following his trade as a carpenter ever since; at this he made a great deal of money." These descriptions of the commercial activities in Santa Fe peaked the interest of Americans living in the river towns of Missouri. By land, Santa Fe was only half as far from Missouri as it was from the Mexican capital. If Pike could cross the Great Plains to Santa Fe, then it should be possible for trading caravans to do the same thing.

The Spanish were suspicious, if not hostile, toward foreigners—but there were rumors of a Mexican rebellion against Spain. By 1812 news of the Hidalgo Revolt reached Missouri and a small group of traders started for Santa Fe, hoping that a new Mexican government would welcome their trade. They followed the general route which Pike described along the Arkansas River. Unfortunately before they arrived in Santa Fe, Miguel Hidalgo had been executed and the rebellion had been crushed. The American traders, Robert McKnight, James Baird, and Samuel Chambers, spent the next nine years in Spanish prisons. They were not released until the successful Iturbide Revolution which finally brought Mexican independence in September 1821.

Meanwhile, the first major financial crisis hit the United States between 1819 and 1821. The Panic of 1819 was followed by bank failures, economic recession, and widespread unemployment. One Missouri businessman, William Becknell, was facing bankruptcy and a jail sentence. In a bold and risky move, he decided to load several mules with trade goods, cross the prairie to Santa Fe, and attempt to sell his wares at a profit. Becknell arrived at Santa Fe in November 1821, and the Mexican people eagerly purchased his goods. His risk paid off and by January 1822 he was back in Missouri with saddlebags full of Mexican silver. He immediately planned a second expedition which left in May, this time using wagons instead of pack animals to haul trade goods. In using this method of transportation, William Becknell became known as the "Father of the Santa Fe Trail."

Mule-drawn freight wagons on the Great Plains.
Courtesy of Library of Congress Photographs Division.

By the mid-1820s the Santa Fe trade had become very lucrative. Senator Thomas Hart Benton of Missouri began promoting the idea of a government sanctioned road to New Mexico, and in 1825 Congress appropriated funds for an official survey of the route. George Sibley and Joseph Brown spent the next two years conducting the survey, laying out the route to take full advantage of available sources of water in the area, and negotiating treaties with Indians on the eastern plains.

No treaties were in place with the tribes of the western and southern plains, however, and in 1829 Major Bennett Riley was dispatched to provide a US military escort for trading caravans. Riley was the first to use oxen for pulling wagons on the Santa Fe Trail, because they were stronger and sturdier even if they were slower. Military escorts were only allowed within US territory, so caravans relied on their own paramilitary forces for protection during the most dangerous southern sections of their journey. In 1833 Charles and William Bent, with their partner Ceran St. Vrain, established a large adobe fort on the Arkansas River for the purpose of trading with the Indians, resupplying wagon

Ox-drawn wagon train crossing the Santa Fe Trail.
Courtesy of Denver Public Library Western History Collection: X-21874.

trains, and sheltering travelers on the trail. At the time, this private fort was the last settlement in US territory, since Bent's Fort was located on the international border with Mexico.

From the very beginning the trail was a commercial trade route, rather than an emigrant's road like the Oregon Trail to the north. The isolated prairie was not a destination, but something to be traversed in order to reach the ultimate endpoint at Santa Fe. There were many hazards of traveling so far from civilization across the Great Plains, including inclement weather, equipment malfunction, dangerous wildlife, hostile Indians, lack of food and water, as well as political difficulties that arose between nations. Despite these hazards, over the years the Santa Fe trade became a thriving commercial enterprise involving thousands of travelers and hundreds of thousands of dollars in revenue.

The Santa Fe Trail was not a single road but consisted of several different routes, each of which cut wide swaths of intersecting paths across the prairie. The Mountain Branch of the trail followed the Arkansas and then the Purgatory River to the point where it met the Sangre de Cristo Mountains. The trail climbed this range to the south by following Raton Creek. After descending Raton Pass, it entered the Cimarron country and hugged the edge of the mountain canyons to the southwest until it reached the Cimarron River. From there the trail turned south, paralleling the mountains until it left the Cimarron country, eventually rounding the southern spur of the Sange de Cristo Mountains, and finally turning northwest to reach Santa Fe.

As traffic increased, outposts grew up along the route at key points where wood and water were readily available, or where crops and livestock could be raised and supplied to travelers. One of the first south-bound stops in the Cimarron country was Willow Springs, a plentiful water source near the site of present-day Raton. Another small settlement grew up several miles south of Willow Springs at the crossing of the Canadian River, where Tom Stockton would eventually build the Clifton House to meet the needs of travelers on the trail. The next reliable source of water was about eleven miles to the southwest on Crow Creek, where another small outpost was created. Eleven miles further to the southwest brought the traveler to the larger Vermejo River, with more plentiful wood and water.

Ponil Creek and the more reliable Cimarron River were twelve miles beyond the Vermejo. In time this would become the largest settlement in the area, where Lucien Maxwell would build his headquarters. Here the trail turned south along the mountains, and within a few miles another small outpost was located on Cimarroncito Creek. The Rayado River was eight miles further to the south, where plenty of wood, water, and game were available. In many of these places livestock and crops also could be raised, so they were ideal locations for frontiersmen to establish small outposts along the trail. Later the owners of the Mexican land grants would encourage and support these settlements because it helped them show progress toward colonization of the area.

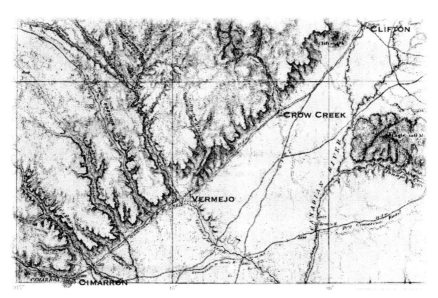

1877 US government survey map showing the Cimarron, Vermejo, Crow Creek, and Clifton House settlements along the Santa Fe Trail near the mouths of the canyons.
Courtesy of Library of Congress Geography and Map Division.

During the mid-1830s trouble developed between the United States and Mexico over the treatment of Texas. Until 1836 Texas had been a Mexican province, colonized primarily by Americans through an agreement with the government of Mexico. In that year, however, the residents revolted and declared Texas to be an independent nation. Armed conflict resulted and the Texans managed to defeat the Mexican army, capturing President Santa Anna and forcing him to recognize Texas independence. Hostilities continued periodically between Texas and Mexico, and the Texans made several attempts to negotiate annexation with the United States. It was not until the end of 1845 that the annexation of Texas became official and it was admitted as a state. This immediately provoked conflict between the United States and Mexico.

In 1846 Colonel Stephen W. Kearney dispatched his "Army of the West" to New Mexico over the Santa Fe Trail. They chose the mountain branch of the trail, via Bent's Fort over Raton Pass and into the Cimarron country. Frontiersmen predicted that there would be little resistance to the US Army, and this proved to be true. On August 15, 1846, Santa Fe was captured without a shot being fired. The official end of the Mexican War did not occur until early in 1848, and military communication became increasingly important during this time.

Many well-known frontiersmen in the Cimarron country were commissioned to carry military dispatches as well as the US mail. In 1846 Thomas Boggs led a party eastbound from Santa Fe with mail for Fort Leavenworth, Kansas, returning to Santa Fe early in 1847. Solomon Sublette left Fort Leavenworth in January 1847 with dispatches for Santa Fe, and he returned with the US mail in April. It is said that Kit Carson carried the first US mail from the Pacific coast to Washington DC along the Santa Fe Trail in the spring of 1848.

In 1849 a US post office was established in Santa Fe, and in 1850 the first mail delivery contract was awarded to pioneering Santa Fe trader David Waldo and his partners from Independence, Missouri. Waldo, Hall, and Company was primarily a freight company and statistics for their business on the Santa Fe Trail provide insights into typical freighting traffic. On July 26, 1850, forty-five of their wagons left Fort Leavenworth carrying almost 250,000 pounds of army supplies to Santa Fe. During that year 154 of their wagons traversed the Santa Fe Trail. It is not surprising that they won the bid on a four-year contract to deliver mail once a month between Independence and Santa Fe, for an annual government stipend of $18,000.

After New Mexico became part of the United States, people were attracted to the territory for a variety of reasons. As a result, better communication and transportation were needed throughout the region. In addition to mail deliveries, passenger traffic also increased along the Santa Fe Trail and regular stagecoach services were established to handle the demand. During the next decade the typical passenger fare from the Missouri settlements to Santa Fe was around $100. Travelers usually slept on the ground with the teamsters, and they cooked their meals around campfires. The wagons or coaches were typically crowded, cramped, and uncomfortable. At sites where stage stations were available, often the beds were hard and the meals were unappetizing. In order to meet strict schedules the coaches kept running day and night, only stopping to change horses or drivers, and this made stage travel a rather miserable experience.

Stagecoach in the Cimarron country around 1870.
Courtesy of W.A. White Collection, Raton Museum.

The Santa Fe Trail became even more dangerous during the Civil War. Indian hostilities increased because soldiers were occupied elsewhere, and many people feared that Confederate troops would raid military and commercial caravans. These circumstances led to a change in traffic on the trail. The more direct dry route across the Oklahoma panhandle was abandoned in favor of the more protected mountain branch through the Cimarron country. In 1861 the US mail route was officially changed to use this section of the trail, and in 1862 the mountain route was used by the 1st Colorado Infantry as it marched to Fort Union and the Battle of Glorieta Pass.

For quite some time well-known frontiersman "Uncle Dick" Wootton had planned to create a better road over Raton Pass. In 1865 he finally obtained charters from both Colorado and New Mexico to build his "inter-territorial highway."

> Barlow and Sanderson, the proprietors of the Santa Fe stage line, were anxious to change their route so as to pass through Trinidad, and freighters generally wanted to come through that way. How to get through the pass was the problem. What I proposed to do was to go into this winding, rock-ribbed mountain pass and hew out a road which, barring grades, should be as good as the average turnpike. I expected to keep this road in good repair and charge a toll for traveling over it, and thought I could see a good business ahead of me... When the stage company commenced running its coaches over my toll road, my place was made a stage station. Of course I had to keep a hotel then, and I entertained guests of all grades and stations, from the Vice President of the United States down to plain stage robbers and horse thieves.

Wootton built a ranch on the Colorado side of Raton Pass, where he lived until just before his death in 1893. His toll road was a financial success from the moment it opened, and it made the mountain route of the Santa Fe Trail more accessible for all vehicles and travelers.

In 1867 rancher Tom Stockton built a three-story adobe structure near the crossing of the Canadian River, calling it the Clifton House. It immediately became one of the most popular overnight stage stations in the Cimarron country. Stockton had windows and furnishings shipped to the site over the Santa Fe Trail, and the building contained large parlors and dining areas with high ceilings, as well as sleeping rooms with individual fireplaces. Cooks and waiters served the guests,

Barlow, Sanderson, and Company stage office in Cimarron.
Courtesy of Old Mill Museum.

and eventually the settlement grew to include a trading post, black-smith shop, and post office.

The village of Cimarron had been granted a US post office on the mail route in 1861, and it too grew into a popular overnight stop for travelers on the Santa Fe Trail. It was already a key freighting destination since it supplied flour, grain, and livestock to US troops stationed in the area. Unusual spring weather in 1867 brought a fierce twelve-hour windstorm, which reportedly blew the stage driver from his seat and required that the coach be chained to the ground to keep it up-right. In 1868 the Barlow and Sanderson stage line maintained an of-fice in Cimarron, running daily service through Cimarron Canyon to Virginia City and Elizabethtown, and from there to Taos once a week.

Rayado was also an important stage stop, providing food and lodg-ing to weary travelers, and in later years it had a US post office. In 1874 an itinerant Methodist preacher, Reverend Thomas Harwood, stopped at the station for the night. He wrote the following letter to his wife, Emily, sharing some of his experiences at Rayado.

> I am tired tonight and hungry, too, and provoked to hear the landlord say, "No supper till the stage comes," and to hear another say, "The stage won't be in till ten o'clock." I should go to bed at once, but who could sleep with all this racket! And besides that, it isn't very pleas-ant to go to bed without supper after a horseback ride of forty miles. To pass the time I would write a little, but saddle bags were stolen and I have no way of carrying stationery. But here comes the land-lord—perhaps he can furnish it. Paper, pen, and ink are furnished and here I sit on a three-legged stool, dirt floor, over by the window, which by the way is my writing desk. This little Mexi-can town, Rayado, is situated on a small mountain stream of the same name. The word is from *rayar*, and signifies a ray or beaming light. This definition agrees well with the light sparkling appearance of the stream, but not to the appearance of the little town. The bell rang for supper. I am glad I made no complaint about a late supper, for I heard the landlady say that she was "tired almost to death, that she had to do about all of her work her-self, that her feet were blistered and worn out walking." She is the only American

Rev. Harwood's window ledge writing desk as it looks today at the restored Rayado stage station.

woman in the place. She, like most American women in this country, has to do her own work.

After the Maxwell Land Grant was purchased by British investors, their managers negotiated lucrative contracts with Barlow and Sanderson to lease the Crow Creek area as a stage station and to provide livestock feed for all of their locations on grant property. The stage company also agreed to pay a reported $2,600 each year to house one of their employees and to lease a stable for eight animals at Cimarron.

During this period the Barlow and Sanderson stage line built a good reputation for keeping their schedules, as well as for the skill of their employees and the quality of their equipment. Their livestock were highly regarded, but they proved to be a vulnerable part of the operation when a tragic illness began to ravage the horses and mules in 1873. It took several months before regular stage and mail service could be resumed. On the eastern parts of the Santa Fe Trail, the railroad's "iron horse" proved to be immune to the disease.

Throughout the 1870s the ever-lengthening railroad lines through Kansas and Colorado territories began to shrink the stage routes. At each new railhead, the stage companies established new offices and plotted new paths over the prairie. For example, when the Kansas Pacific Railroad built the town of Kit Carson in Colorado, the stage line was adjusted to run south toward the Arkansas River where it connected with the mountain branch of the Santa Fe Trail.

Freight and stage companies scrambled to maintain their routes and revenue as the railroads began to take over their services along the main line. The Barlow and Sanderson company focused on developing stage service into the mountain settlements where there would be little competition from the railroads. In several places there were min-

Freight wagons being loaded from train cars at a railroad station.

Courtesy of Library of Congress Photographs Division.

ing boom towns, especially in the Baldy Mountain area, and the stage lines quickly expanded their service into those locations. By this time, however, the stage lines were no more than spurs off the main railroad route through the eastern edge of the Cimarron country.

On July 4, 1879, the Santa Fe Railroad reached Las Vegas, New Mexico. In early 1880 the Las Vegas *Gazette* printed the following poignant news item about the abandonment of the Santa Fe Trail, which had been made obsolete by the coming of the railroad.

> Yesterday morning the last stagecoach left Las Vegas for Santa Fe. We are sorry to see them go. The stage men and employees looked like they were leaving their earthly treasures. This stage line was a great and ancient institution. It came in after General Kearny's army in 1846. At first it was a mail every six months brought through under guard. The service was soon increased to monthly and finally to daily, and prior to the railroads these were halcyon days. Gradually the iron horse has been driven down the Santa Fe Trail, and at each extension it shortened the stage line. Now it is reduced to a short 15-mile run, to disappear forever in another week. It will be an institution of the past, but will always be remembered by the old inhabitants of New Mexico.

A Mexican Land Grant Shapes the Cimarron Country

At the height of the controversy over land ownership in the Cimarron country, the Santa Fe *Daily New Mexican* newspaper of April 19, 1887, made a very profound statement about the Maxwell Land Grant: "The history of this grant is the history of New Mexico." This claim may be a bit broad, but it certainly was true that the history of the Cimarron country was tied to this Mexican land grant. It was a time of transition between several different traditions, rules, and laws controlling the use of property. Native people groups had one view of the land, while Spanish and Mexican colonizers had quite another. Ultimately the land came under the jurisdiction of American property laws, adding yet another transition as well as a period of upheaval and unrest for residents of the land.

From the very beginning the Mexican land grants were colored by contention and political wrangling. The story of the grant which encompassed the Cimarron country begins with a Canadian-born merchant who settled in Taos and became a naturalized Mexican citizen. Charles Hipolyte Trotier inherited his French family title "Sieur de Beaubien." When he arrived in New Mexico in 1823 he chose to be known as Carlos Beaubien. After settling in Taos he

Carlos Beaubien
Courtesy of Philmont Scout Ranch.

By Steve Lewis

married Maria Paula Lobato, the daughter of a prominent Mexican family. Over the next several decades Beaubien became one of the most influential citizens on the northern frontier of the Mexican Republic.

Beaubien was an educated and intelligent man who was concerned for the people of the area. He was also an astute businessman with an ambition for prosperity and personal betterment. In 1840 he created a plan for developing a large tract of unused land, not only for its economic rewards but also for the improvement of the residents of northern New Mexico. Beaubien realized that even though he had been a naturalized citizen for almost two decades, in some quarters he still would be viewed as an outsider because of his foreign birth. In order to increase his chance of success, he enlisted a well-known Mexican government official, Guadalupe Miranda, as his partner in the project.

On January 8, 1841, Beaubien and Miranda petitioned governor Manuel Armijo for a grant of land northeast of Taos. One of their reasons for requesting the grant was to develop the rich natural resources on the northern frontier.

> Of all the departments in the republic, with the exception of the Californias, New Mexico is one of the most backward in intelligence, industry, manufactories, etc, and surely few others present the natural advantages to be found therein, not only on account of its abundance of water, forests, wood, and useful timber, but also on account of the fertility of the soil, containing within its bosom rich and precious metals, which up to this time are useless for the want of enterprising men who will convert them to the advantages of other men, all of which productions of nature are susceptible of being used for the benefit of society in the department as well as in the entire republic, if they were in the hands of individuals who would work and improve them...If the fertile lands of New Mexico are not reduced to private property, where it will be improved, it will be of no benefit to the department.

This reasoning has a familiar ring to it, because so many men before and since have focused on acquiring private property in order to exploit the bounty of the land. However, Beaubien and Miranda went on to explain their plan for the betterment of the Mexican people.

> The department abounds in idle people, who for the want of occupation, are a burden to the industrious portion of society...Idleness, the mother of vice, is the cause of the increase of crimes which are daily being committed...The towns are overrun with thieves and murderers who by this means alone desire to procure their subsistence.

They desired to provide honest employment for idle men, and their hope was that this would raise the moral tone of the entire society. In addition to this, Beaubien and Miranda saw benefit in protecting the northern frontier as well as reducing the need for foreign aid by making the area more self-sufficient.

> The welfare of a nation consists in the possession of lands which produce all the necessaries of life without requiring those of other nations, and it cannot be denied that New Mexico possesses this great advantage and only requires industrious hands to make it a happy residence.

Their simple plan was to obtain a grant of land "for the purpose of improving it, without injury to any third party, and raising sugar beets, which we believe will grow well and produce an abundant crop, and in time to establish manufactories of cotton and wool, and raising stock of every description." The final paragraph of their request outlined the boundaries of the proposed tract of land in very general terms, which was the common practice of that time. Three days later the governor approved their request and unconditionally granted all of the land they requested.

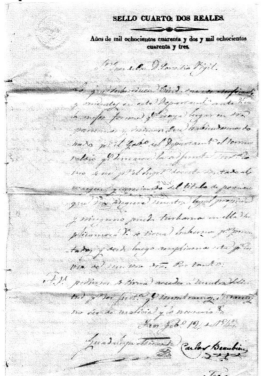

Signature page from the 1841 Mexican land grant, showing the signatures of Guadalupe Miranda & Carlos Beaubien.

Courtesy of New Mexico State Records Center and Archives.

SANM I, Collection 1972-007, Series V, Subseries 5.2, Item SG 15, Beaubien and Miranda Grant.

During the intervening year, apparently Beaubien and Miranda explored the property and created a plat map which showed the boundaries of their grant in more specific terms. In February 1843 they appeared before the justice of the peace in Taos to request official title to their land under local law.

> Having received from the government of the department a grant to the public land set forth in the accompanying plat, and having no title of possession which will secure our legal property and prevent anyone from disturbing us in it, we request you to execute the [title] to be used according to our rights.

The following day Justice Cornelio Vigil agreed to travel to the property with Beaubien and Miranda so that "the possession solicited be given to the petitioners, in order that it may be held by them, their heirs and successors, according to law." On February 22nd they began to build a series of seven mounds that marked the perimeter of the grant, and Vigil performed the ceremony then common in Mexico for giving title to a tract of land.

> I took them by the hand, walked with them, caused them to throw earth, pull up weeds, and show other evidences of possession, with which the act was concluded, the boundaries being determined without any claim whatsoever to the injury of any third party.

In order to begin developing the property, Beaubien requested help from his associates in Taos to start colonizing the grant. Bent, St. Vrain & Company was active in the Taos trade and maintained several outposts along the Santa Fe Trail. They agreed to build structures and cultivate land at several key points within the grant—notably, at Vermejo, Ponil, and Cimarron. In 1843 even Taos justice of the peace Cornelio Vigil was recruited to settle along the Cimarron River. Kit Carson later testified, "I passed there in 1844 with Lucien B. Maxwell and saw large fields of corn, beans, pumpkins, and a great deal of land cultivated, and several houses built on the big Cimarron."

From Vigil's official title document it is clear that early in 1843 there had been no opposition to the land grant. However, later that year the local village priest, Father Antonio José Martinez, with the support of Indians from the Taos Pueblo, protested against the grant. He claimed that the land could not be given to Beaubien because he was a foreigner, and that the grant included protected Indian grazing and hunting grounds. Early in 1844 the new acting governor, Mariano

Chavez, reviewed the documents, agreed with Martinez, and suspended the grant. By that time many colonists had built houses and planted crops on the property.

Beaubien immediately responded with an appeal, pointing out the errors and contradictions in the complaint by Father Martinez. Beaubien also presented a "long list of persons to whom they have offered land for cultivation." In April 1844 the current governor referred the case to the Departmental Assembly, which consisted of prominent citizens and government officials. They determined that the order of suspension had been based on false statements, and that the original grant was completely legitimate.

> It is well known and certain that it has never been used as pasture grounds for cattle, and that for a long time it has not been used for hunting buffaloes. On the contrary the settlement of that place would be a benefit to the interior settlements, affording them protection from the enemy in that direction, occupying a great number of idlers who have no occupation in the cultivation of the soil, and relieving this vicinity from a large number of persons who crowd us. The endless difficulties we experience every year on account of the scarcity of water for irrigation would be avoided.

The Departmental Assembly was enthusiastically in favor of colonizing the grant for at least three reasons: It would provide a protective buffer from northern enemies, it would give productive jobs to idle men, and it would relieve the overcrowded conditions in populated areas. On April 18, 1844, the governor proclaimed, "The order of the 27th of February forbidding the free use of the land in question is repealed, and Messrs. Beaubien and Miranda are fully authorized to establish their colony."

Kit Carson and Lucien Maxwell built adobe homes on the Rayado.
Courtesy of Philmont Scout Ranch.

In 1845 Kit Carson and Richard Owens established a settlement along Cimarroncito Creek south of the Cimarron River. Around this time Thomas Boggs and John Hatcher also built homes and cultivated fields along Ponil Creek. In *Wah-to-Yah and the Taos Trail* Lewis Garrard wrote from the Ponil area that, "Grizzly bear are plenty in this vicinity…Hatcher and Boggs built cabins near here, with the intention of farming. To protect their corn from these bold predators, they erected scaffolds in the fields from which they could fight off the marauders." Through 1846 George Bent and Ceran St. Vrain continued to raise cattle in the Vermejo and Cimarroncito areas.

The war between the United States and Mexico began in 1846, and the American occupation of New Mexico again changed the legal landscape for grant owners. Both Manuel Armijo and Guadalupe Miranda fled south into Mexico, leaving Beaubien to sort out issues with the title to the property. Also, during the Taos Rebellion in January 1847, many of Beaubien's closest relatives, associates, and partners were murdered. He turned to his son-in-law, Lucien B. Maxwell, to carry on the work of colonizing the grant. Early in 1848 Maxwell led a party to the Rayado River, including Tim Goodale, Manuel LeFavre, and James White. By 1849 Kit Carson had joined Maxwell on the Rayado, but in that year James White and his family were killed by hostile Indians.

Despite continued attacks by Indians, the Rayado ranch prospered. Beginning in 1850, and periodically for several years afterward, companies of US soldiers were stationed at Rayado to protect the settlement as well as travelers on the Santa Fe Trail. By 1855 Rayado was a thriving colony, and in 1857 Lucien Maxwell decided to develop a larger ranch along the Cimarron River to the north.

This was the same year that Beaubien and Miranda petitioned the US government to confirm their title to the grant under the terms of the Treaty of Guadalupe Hidalgo. Their lawyers claimed that "they have cultivated and improved portions of said land for the last twelve years, whereby it has become of great value, and they are still cultivating and improving the same." After reviewing all of the original documents and hearing the testimony of many witnesses, US Surveyor General William Pelham rendered the final decision.

> The grant having been confirmed by the departmental assembly and been in the constant occupation of the grantees from the date of the grant until the present time, as is proven by the testimony of witnesses, it is the opinion of this office that it is a good and valid

grant according to the laws and customs of the government of the republic of Mexico and the decisions of the Supreme Court of the United States, as well as the treaty of Guadalupe Hidalgo, and is therefore confirmed to Charles Beaubien and Guadalupe Miranda, and is transmitted for the action of Congress.

Guadalupe Miranda never returned to northern New Mexico, and in 1858 he sold his interest in the grant to Lucien Maxwell for about $2,500. On June 21, 1860, after a delay of over two years, the US Congress confirmed the 1857 ruling of the Surveyor General and established the validity of the grant under American law. Carlos Beaubien died in 1864, and Maxwell immediately began purchasing the shares of the grant held by Beaubien's heirs. By 1865 he had become the majority owner of the grant, and it eventually became known as the Maxwell Land Grant.

The government had established the Ute and Apache Indian agency at Cimarron in 1861, so four years later in 1865 Maxwell offered to sell the entire grant for $250,000 to the government for use as an Indian reservation. In the wake of the Civil War and in view of current conditions on the frontier, government officials declined Maxwell's offer. In 1866 gold was discovered in the mountains on the western edge of the grant, and Maxwell would reap great economic rewards for developing the area. He established sawmills, water ditch projects, and platted towns for the sale of commercial and residential property. He owned several of the largest mines in the Baldy area, and during the next few years he developed those properties by constructing stamp mills to process the gold ore.

It was reported that by 1868 Lucien Maxwell was one of the wealthiest men in New Mexico. Revenue came from a variety of sources. He received income from government contracts for feeding the Indians

Maxwell's Aztec grist mill provided flour for the Cimarron Indian Agency.

Courtesy of Library of Congress Photographs Division.

and providing goods to soldiers in the area, from the sale of livestock and grain to local settlers, from leases for mining properties and from gold processed in his Baldy mines, from the sale of lumber and town lots on which to build, from leases for water delivered through his irrigation ditches, as well as from goods and services provided to travelers along the Santa Fe Trail. Maxwell had made a huge commercial success of the land grant, but it was becoming increasingly complicated for him to manage. Maxwell began searching for a buyer.

In 1869 he negotiated with three Colorado investors, Jerome B. Chaffee, George M. Chilcott, and Charles F. Holly. In May of that year Maxwell gave them an option to buy the grant, and he immediately commissioned a survey of the property. William W. Griffin was contracted by the Surveyor General's office and he completed the project based on the original boundary descriptions, filing his documentation with the General Land Office in Santa Fe by late 1869.

When the survey was almost complete, Secretary of the Interior Jacob D. Cox heard of the project and disputed it. He ruled that "where a Mexican colonization grant is confirmed without measurement of boundaries...no greater than eleven square leagues shall be surveyed." Maxwell's lawyers submitted a lengthy rebuttal, but by this time the survey had already been filed as if it were officially sanctioned. Meanwhile the three investors holding the purchase option were marketing the grant as if the title were clear.

Early in 1870 they negotiated a new agreement to purchase Maxwell's holdings for a reported $1,350,000. They immediately assigned their option to the Maxwell Land Grant and Railway Company, which completed the purchase on behalf of a group of British investors. They took ownership of the property and attempted to collect rent from residents whom they considered 'squatters' on their land. In past years, Maxwell had often allowed people to live rent-free on the grant, taking payment in a portion of their crops or livestock. Under the new ownership, however, none of those previous arrangements were considered valid.

Resentment ran high, and residents organized 'squatters clubs' to unite for the purpose of determining what should be done. There were scattered incidents of violence when company employees attempted to move settlers off their farms. Many homesteaders believed they had 'proved up' their right to the land under the Homestead Act of 1862, since they had made improvements and occupied the property for at least five years. They considered the actions of the company to be illegal, and they hired attorneys to sue the company in hopes of challenging its claims in court. Based on Secretary Cox's ruling, the settlers claimed ownership of their land unless the company could show a valid survey that specifically proved otherwise.

In 1871 lawyers for the Maxwell Land Grant company petitioned the new Secretary of the Interior, Columbus Delano, to order an official government survey of the grant. The company deposited the required funds for the survey with the General Land Office. After reviewing the grant documents for many months, Secretary Delano decided not to become involved in the dispute. He stood behind Secretary Cox's previous ruling and declared that if government officials were to reverse each other's decisions, then controversies like this might continue unresolved indefinitely. The company then requested that their funds be returned, and apparently they determined to pursue their own private survey of the property.

When Willis Drummond, commissioner of the General Land Office in 1874, learned about this he ordered what amounted to an annulment of the grant and declared that it should be treated as public land open to settlement. He instructed the Surveyor General at Santa Fe, "As the claimants have withdrawn their whole deposit and refused to comply with the terms of the decision, you will regard and treat the lands claimed by them as public lands and extend the public surveys over the same." This action exceeded his legal authority when dealing with a land grant previously confirmed by Congress, and it multiplied the confusion surrounding land ownership in the Cimarron country.

The Maxwell Land Grant company continued to deal with residents under the assumption that it owned the grant, but at the same time the General Land Office began issuing deeds to settlers on the same property which it considered public domain. Violence again broke out in 1875 when an outspoken opponent of the company, Reverend Franklin J. Tolby, was found murdered in Cimarron Canyon. This touched off a series of murders and violence during what be-

Reverend Franklin J. Tolby
Courtesy of Quentin Robinson Collection.

came known as the Colfax County War.

In 1876 the US Supreme Court heard the landmark case of *John Tameling v. United States Freehold & Immigration Company*. This case involved the Sangre de Cristo Land Grant, which was a sister grant to the Maxwell Land Grant. Like the settlers in the Cimarron country, Tameling had claimed a 160-acre homestead on grant property. The Supreme Court found in favor of the grant owners, however, and ruled that a Mexican grant which had been confirmed by Congress was not limited in size, but should be surveyed and patented according to the geographical boundaries given in the original documents.

Based on this new legal precedent, in March 1877 the Maxwell Land Grant Company resubmitted its petition for the government to survey and patent its holdings. Land commissioner J. A. Williamson ordered the survey, and within a month it had been completed and filed with the land office. It was not until almost two years later, on

Patent map of the Maxwell Land Grant

Courtesy of History Colorado Center: T.A. Schomburg Collection.

May 19, 1879, that the patent was issued for a total of 1,714,764.94 acres of land. Over the years the Maxwell Land Grant Company had endured several periods of financial instability, brought on at least in part by uncertainties about its title to the property, so this official patent was a welcome relief to the company.

Even though the company now held a legal patent to the grant, opposition to its ownership continued. Reverend Oscar P. McMains, a colleague of the late Reverend Tolby, took up the cause after Tolby's death. McMains devoted the rest of his life to opposing the claims of the Maxwell Land Grant Company, and in 1881 he traveled to Washington to ask Secretary of the Interior Samuel J. Kirkwood to reexamine the patent. Kirkwood declined, but in 1882 McMains convinced the new US Attorney General that there were grounds for invalidating the patent. In August of that year Attorney General Benjamin H. Brewster filed a cancellation lawsuit in the US 8th Circuit Court in Denver.

Pretrial hearings, briefs, depositions, and counter-motions occurred over the next three years until the case finally came to trial before Judge David J. Brewer late in 1885. The decision was announced in January 1886, with the court ruling in favor of the Maxwell Land Grant Company. By this time the Justice Department had invested several years in this effort, so they appealed the decision to the US Supreme Court where the case was argued in March 1887. One of the key factors in the final decision was expressed by Justice Samuel Miller.

> The case before us is much stronger than the ordinary case of an attempt to set aside a patent, or even the judgment of a court, because it demands of us that we shall disregard or annul the deliberate action of the congress of the United States. The constitution declares that 'the congress shall have power to dispose of and make all needful rules and regulations respecting the territory or other property belonging to the United States.' At the time the congress passed upon the grant to Beaubien and Miranda...it was the property of the United States, and congress confirmed the grant. It is not easy to perceive how the courts of the United States can set aside this action of congress.

The court found no basis for falsification, misrepresentation, or error in the official survey of the property, stating that "there is an utter failure to establish either mistake or fraud." Their final decision, handed down on April 18, 1887, was that "for these reasons the decree of the circuit court is affirmed." The Maxwell Land Grant had been successfully defended in the nation's highest court.

McMains was desperate to annul the grant and he traveled to Washington for one last appeal to President Grover Cleveland. Cleveland's response was clear and direct: "The judgment of the Supreme Court is authoritative and conclusive. Its judgment must be respected and obeyed." This seemed to be the final nail in the coffin of anti-grant activism, although McMains continued the futile fight through the local newspapers until his death in 1899.

In order to put the Maxwell Land Grant Company on a better financial footing, the managers restructured the company in 1888, with new bonds that would come due in 1920. Frank Springer became president and immediately began developing the company's resources, including the sale of land, town development, livestock production, timber leases, irrigation projects, and mining of coal and other precious minerals. Through these efforts he was able to make the company profitable enough to pay the interest on its bonds, culminating in the successful dissolution of the Maxwell Land Grant trust around the time of Springer's death in 1927. The remaining property held by Dutch owners was sold off until it was gone by the early 1960s.

Today the Cimarron country is a relatively quiet and peaceful place, and the property is secure in the hands of private, public, or corporate owners. These lands were shaped by this Mexican land grant, but there are many more stories to tell about the incredible events which were to take place throughout the Cimarron country.

Pioneer Ranch on the Rayado

Kit Carson says in his memoirs that in April 1849 he and Lucien Maxwell "concluded to make a settlement at the Rayado. We felt we had been leading a roving life long enough and that now, if ever, was the time to make a home for ourselves and children. We were getting old [he was 40 years old at the time] and could not expect much longer to continue to gain a livelihood as we had been doing for many years. So we went to Rayado, where we commenced building and making other improvements, and were soon started on the way to prosperity."

Carson and Maxwell had pursued long and distinguished careers in the mountains and on the plains as beaver trappers, hunters, and scouts in the American West. They had become close friends several years earlier when they rode with Lieutenant John C. Fremont on his first exploring expedition of the West in 1842. When Maxwell was sent to colonize his father-in-law Carlos Beaubien's Mexican land grant in 1848, he naturally invited his friend to share in the enterprise.

Beaubien and Guadalupe Miranda had received the land grant in 1841. Frontier conditions, however, precluded settlement until the spring of 1848 when Maxwell led colonists from Taos over the mountains to the grant. The Rayado River, where it flows eastward onto the plains from the Sangre de Cristo Mountains, was selected for the site of the colony not only because of its good water and lush pastures, but

From "Kit Carson and Lucien Maxwell's Pioneer Ranch" by Stephen Zimmer, *Wild West*, Vol. 13, No. 4, December 2000: 50-54, 80.

because it lay only a few miles north of where a trail branched off the Santa Fe Trail over the mountains to Taos.

The first description of Maxwell and Carson's ranch was recorded by Charles Pancoast who stopped there in July 1849. Traveling the Santa Fe Trail with a group destined for the goldfields of California, Pancoast noted in his diary that the "ranch house could not be said to be stylish: it was a two-story log affair, surrounded by adobe walls for purposes of fortification. Inside the walls were several adobe houses, and outside a number more, as well as a large corral and several buildings used as stables, slaughter houses, etc." Pancoast wrote that a "dozen or more Americans and Mexicans" resided at the ranch along with twenty Indians from various tribes.

Like many who met Kit Carson, Pancoast was intrigued with the famous mountain man. He described him as having dark skin, and "he wore his long black hair over his coat, giving him much the appearance of a Mexican. He dressed in first class Indian style in buckskin coat and pants trimmed with leather dangles, and wore moccasins on his feet and Mexican sombrero on his head."

Carson was cordial to the gold-seekers and gave them beef to cook for supper. At the beginning of the visit he said little to them until they had eaten. Then he came to sit at their campfire, and Pancoast reported that he became "very garrulous, entertaining us until eleven o'clock with his numerous Indian adventures. He spoke of the difficulties he had experienced in maintaining the lonely position he occupied and in protecting his stock from the raids of the Utes and other Indians." The mountaineer even showed them "several arrow and bullet wounds on his person that he had received in his encounters with the Indians, in which he gloried as much as could the most distinguished General."

As Carson had recounted, the Rayado settlement suffered repeated Indian attacks from its inception. The indigenous Utes and Jicarilla Apaches not only coveted the ranchers' herds of cattle, horses, mules, and sheep, but resented the settlers' encroachment on their land as well. Several Rayado residents were to fall victim to Apache and Ute arrows and scalping knives in the first years of the settlement.

After moving to the Rayado, Carson was often enlisted by officers stationed in Taos as a scout to rescue Indian captives or retrieve livestock stolen from Rayado or other settlements. A few months after his arrival at Rayado, a party of Santa Fe traders under the leadership of J.M. White was attacked by Apaches eighty miles east of the settlement. White and several others were killed in the attack, while his wife and young daughter were taken captive. In the aftermath of the attack the Indians broke open trunks, cut harness, and destroyed everything they could not carry with them. When news of the attack reached the command in Taos, Captain William S. Grier was dispatched to Rayado with a company of dragoons to pursue the raiders. When the troops reached the ranch, Carson joined them.

For two weeks the soldiers followed Indian trails across the barren plains of northeastern New Mexico Territory. They finally encountered the responsible band of Apaches, and Carson recommend-

*An early sketch of Kit Carson:
"He led the way."*

ed that they immediately be attacked. Instead, Captain Grier halted the party thinking that the Indians wished to parley. As he did, a shot was fired from the Indian camp. Grier was struck in the chest but was miraculously saved from injury when the ball hit the leather gauntlets he carried inside his coat.

After recovering from the impact of the bullet, Grier ordered the troops to charge. Because the Indians had been given time enough to make their escape, only one Indian was killed. As the soldiers searched the Indians' camp, Mrs. White was found dead, having been shot with an arrow only moments before. No evidence of her daughter was found.

In his memoirs Carson stated how much he lamented Mrs. White's death. "I am certain that if the Indians had been charged immediately on our arrival, she would have been saved. The Indians did not know of our approach and perhaps, not paying any particular watch of her, she could have run towards us, the Indians fearing to pursue. She could not possibly have lived long, for the treatment she had received from the Indians was so brutal and horrible that she could possibly last but a short period."

He also stated that a book was found in the Indian camp, "the first of the kind I had ever seen, in which I was made a great hero, slaying Indians by the hundred, and I have often thought that as Mrs. White would read the same, and knowing that I lived near, she would pray for my appearance and that she would be saved, I did come, but had not the power to convince those that were in command over me to pursue my plan for her rescue. They would not listen to me and they failed."

The soldiers gathered what horses the Apaches had abandoned and proceeded to pursue the fleeing Indians. After six miles of hard travel, they again encountered them, slaying one and taking several others prisoner. Feeling that they had sufficiently chastised the Indians, they turned their horses westward and marched back to the Rayado.

The White massacre alerted military officials in New Mexico to the necessity of providing better protection for traders on the Santa Fe Trail. As Rayado was deemed the logical place to station troops, ten mounted dragoons, under the command of Sergeant Leigh Holbrook, were dispatched to the settlement in the winter of 1850.

The following March a party of Indians attacked some herders who were camped about two miles from the ranch. They ran off the herders' horses and mules and severely wounded two of the men. Another herder escaped and successfully made his way back to sound the alarm at the Rayado gates.

The next morning Carson led Sergeant Holbrook and the dragoons to the site of the Indian attack. They found the Indians' trail and followed it at a gallop for twenty-five miles. When they encountered the Indians, they approached cautiously and then charged. Five Indians were killed while several others escaped. Carson's party recovered all but four head of livestock. Commenting on the dragoons' effort from his post in Taos, Captain Grier wrote that he regarded the "affair as a very handsome one and very creditable to the sergeant and his men."

On May 5th Carson and his friend Tim Goodel left Rayado with fifty head of horses and mules destined for trade at Fort Laramie with overland emigrants. They arrived safely in early June, disposing of their "animals to good advantage." Afterward, Goodel left for California, and Carson turned home to the Rayado ranch.

When he reached the Greenhorn settlement on the Arkansas River, he was told to be on the lookout for Indians on the trail to the south. With only one traveling companion, he rode another forty miles and stopped to rest at the Trinchera River. After concealing the riding and

Painting of life at the Rayado settlement.
Courtesy of Philmont Scout Ranch.

pack animals some distance off the road, he took his rifle and climbed a nearby cottonwood tree in order to secure a better vantage point to spot Indians. In his memoirs Carson stated that he "remained in that position during the entire day. Sometimes I would fall asleep, and nearly fall, but would recover in time and continue my watch. Near evening I saw a large body of Indians about one half mile distant."

Fortunately for the mountain man, the Indians did not discover his tree. When they rode out of sight, he dropped from the tree, saddled the horses, and made his escape. He discovered no more Indians on the rest of the trip and reached Rayado by "keeping to the brush some distance off the road."

The ability of the dragoons to successfully defend Rayado prompted the military to establish a more permanent detachment there. Under orders that were issued on May 24, 1850, Captain Grier led Companies G and I of the 1st Dragoons eastward over the mountains to the settlement. The two companies consisted of forty-three men supplied with forty-five horses. Each soldier carried a carbine, and the detachment was equipped with a six-pound cannon and a mountain howitzer.

A few weeks after the soldiers' arrival, the Apaches again attacked Rayado, running off six horses, four mules, and 175 head of cattle.

During the assault the soldiers' bugler was killed when he was caught unarmed outside the compound, as was William New, a mountain man visiting his old friends Carson and Maxwell at the ranch.

This most recent attack convinced military officials that a concerted offensive was necessary to counter the Indian raids. Post Commander Grier, who had been promoted to Brevet Major, was ordered to lead the two companies stationed at Rayado in addition to Company K of the Second Dragoons and about ninety civilians in a retaliatory campaign against the Jicarillas.

The largest force thus far ever mounted against hostiles in the northeastern part of New Mexico Territory rode north from Rayado in late July 1850. When the command reached the Vermejo River, they turned west into the Sangre de Cristo mountains and soon discovered an Indian trail. Encountering a small group of Apaches, they attacked and killed or wounded all of them.

The next day the main camp of Indians was sighted "on the edge of a mountain, in a thick and almost impenetrable growth of aspens." The surrounding area was marshy, which caused Major Grier difficulty in deploying his troops for attack. When he finally brought them into position, the Indians abandoned their camp and fled in small groups further into the mountains. Grier, however, chose not to pursue because of the rough terrain. The attack resulted in only five or six casualties, although the troopers recovered most of the stolen livestock.

The presence of dragoons at Rayado did, however, lessen the regularity of Apache assaults. As a result Maxwell took the opportunity to have his men build a permanent compound for the ranch designed not only to fulfill the need for work, storage, and living areas but to provide necessary protection in case of Indian attack as well.

Once constructed, it was described by a visitor as being "composed of a plaza surrounded by adobe walls eighteen inches thick and eight to ten feet high. Excepting in front the walls are double and far enough apart to furnish a convenient apartment, say twelve feet in width. This plaza is winged by similar small courts, walled in by houses. Adobe corrals for stock, and outdoor ovens of the same material, finish the picture." Later Carson had a similar but smaller compound constructed a quarter of a mile to the south.

With the safety of the settlement assured, Maxwell and Carson were more willing to leave the settlement for extended periods and devote their energies to their ranching enterprise. Their first order of business was to acquire much needed supplies that could only be procured in the Missouri settlements east across the Santa Fe Trail.

Therefore, when the grass began to grow in March 1851, Maxwell sent Carson with twelve ox-drawn wagons east to Missouri. He reached the settlements in early May and soon was back on the trail. On the Arkansas River he encountered a war party of Cheyennes who made a show of attacking his train. Carson, however, persuaded them to parley, and a battle was avoided. With no other incidents, he reached Rayado in June with his freight in good order.

During Carson's absence Maxwell was informed by Colonel E.V. Sumner, commander of the Ninth Military Department of New Mexico, that he felt the increasing number of settlements along the Santa Fe Trail could be more effectively protected by establishing a large force at one strategically located post. Consequently, in mid-May a detachment of troops stationed at Maxwell's was ordered to the Mora River thirty miles south of Rayado for the purpose of erecting a fortification to be called Fort Union. By the end of July all soldiers from Rayado had departed for their new assignment.

In spite of the loss of the dragoon detachment, Carson and Maxwell outfitted a party of eighteen men for a trapping expedition to the headwaters of the Arkansas River. With Carson as leader, the party "went

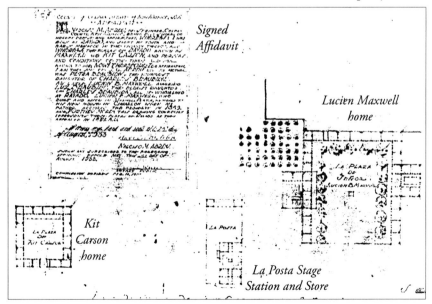

Plat map of the buildings at the original Rayado settlement,
from recollections described by Narciso Abreu, circa 1933.
Courtesy of Philmont Scout Ranch.

to the Balla Salado, then down the South Fork to the Plains, through the Plains of Laramie to the New Park, trapped it to the Old Park, then again to the Balla Salado, then on the Arkansas where it goes out of the mountain, then followed on under the mountain, thence home to the Rayado, through the Raton Mountain." Although the expedition trapped a good supply of beaver, the effort ultimately proved to be unprofitable due to the prevailing low price of fur. It was nonetheless rewarding in that it allowed the two mountaineers and their companions to relive their youthful glory days as beaver trappers.

Some time later when Maxwell and Carson were away from the ranch on a trading expedition, several mounted Apache warriors were spotted one morning on a hill overlooking the ranch. Although a parley was sought, the request was answered with gunfire and the appearance of more than six hundred tribesmen in full war dress. The besieged settlers decided to send a messenger south to Fort Union for help. Vidal Trujillo volunteered for the desperate ride and chose *Rayado*, the fastest horse at the settlement, as his mount. According to one writer, as Trujillo mounted, "the big chestnut horse shot like a thunderbolt into the midst of the savages. So unexpected the act, and so complete the surprise, the flying rider was through the line before the Indians knew what was happening. Fate rode with Vidal that day. Miraculously, he escaped their arrows and by virtue of the great horse under him, outran them." Trujillo rode so hard that the brave horse collapsed in death just as they reached the fort. But in the best tradition of a good Western movie, he arrived in time so that soldiers were able to reach the ranch and thwart the Indians' attack.

Two years afterward Carson and Maxwell embarked on the most ambitious, yet precarious enterprise of their partnership. In February 1853 the two men traveled to the southern part of New Mexico Territory and purchased three herds of sheep consisting of 6,500 each. Their goal was to drive the sheep to California and sell them to feed miners in the burgeoning goldfields. Each man took charge of a herd, while another partner, mountain man John L. Hatcher, bossed the third.

The herds departed a month apart. The trail led north past Rayado and along the foot of the Rockies to Fort Laramie where it intersected the Oregon-California emigrant trail. From there the drovers headed west, eventually crossing Utah, and over the Sierra Nevadas into the California goldfields. The drives took six months each, covered more than 1,500 miles, and resulted in only a few losses. The sheep that had been bought in New Mexico for 50¢ per head were sold in Sacramento for $5.50 each. Consequently, the ranchers rode home to the Rayado via the Gila route of southern Arizona much pleased with their success.

Upon Carson's return, he learned that he had been appointed United States Indian Agent for the Jicarillas and Utes, a position he felt obligated to accept in order to do what he could for the now destitute tribe. The agency headquarters was to be in Taos, so he regretfully packed his belongings and left the Rayado for good.

Maxwell continued at the ranch until 1857 when he decided to move his livestock ten miles north to the mouth of the Cimarron River. The new location had an abundant water supply capable of irrigating the expansive bottom lands there. His farmers soon had fields planted in wheat, corn, barley, and hay while his herders watched over great herds of horses, mules, cattle, and sheep. In addition he filled a mercantile store with an abundance of goods freighted over the Santa Fe Trail, and soon his ranch became the commercial center of the region. A town called Cimarron sprang from this foundation.

The Rayado area came into possession of Maxwell's brother-in-law, Jesus Abreu, who was also married to one of Carlos Beaubien's daughters. With Indian attack no longer a threat, Abreu operated the ranch with great success for the next half century until his death in 1900. Rayado Ranch eventually was acquired by Waite Phillips in 1929, who added it to his sprawling Philmont Ranch west and south of Cimarron.

By 1941 Phillips had given more than 127,000 acres of his ranch to the Boy Scouts of America to serve as a wilderness camping area that became known as Philmont Scout Ranch. In his gift he specifically included the historic structures that remained at Rayado in order that the

Ruins of Kit Carson's home at Rayado, circa 1900.
Courtesy of Philmont Scout Ranch.

organization could use them to tell the story of Carson and Maxwell's exploits in establishing the pioneer New Mexican ranch.

Today, Scouts from all over the United States hike and camp in the mountains west of Cimarron each summer, often walking the same trails that the famous mountain men once rode. Philmont officials refurbished the existing portions of Carson and Maxwell's adobe plazas at Rayado, using historic photographs and original walls and foundation lines. With the help of costumed staff interpreters, Scouts today can learn of Carson and Maxwell's tribulations in establishing the ranch. They come away not only with an appreciation of their heroic efforts, but with an understanding of the difficulty of life experienced by countless pioneer men and women on the western frontier.

Gold on Baldy Mountain

In the summer of 1866 a Ute Indian trading at Ft. Union, New Mexico, showed a "pretty rock" to Captain William H. Moore. The captain recognized it as "rich copper float" which was at the time in great demand in New Mexico. Consequently, he paid the Ute for the specimen and asked if he would show him where he found it. The Ute agreed and guided Moore and a party of soldiers to Baldy Mountain on the west side of Maxwell's land grant.

There they discovered a hillside blanketed with copper ore. In October Moore and his associate, William Kroenig, dispatched Larry Bronson, Pete Kinsinger, and a soldier named Kelley to Baldy to begin assessment work at the copper site and start readying the ore for shipment. The three men camped the first night on the upper reaches of Willow Creek. While Bronson and Kinsinger set up camp and started supper, Kelley took a gold pan and started washing gravel at the creek. Soon he yelled to his camp-mates that he was seeing good color in his pan. Supper was all but forgotten as all three men began sloshing creek gravel in their pans.

For the next few days they panned furiously, but when the snow began to fly, they discontinued their efforts and returned to Ft. Union. Before they left, they marked the big Ponderosa pine that hung over their camp and named it "Discovery Tree."

The three prospectors vowed not to divulge the location of their discovery to anyone. But, human nature being what it is, one, two, or

---

By Stephen Zimmer

Supper was all but forgotten as the men began sloshing creek gravel in their pans near the Discovery Tree.

From *Harper's Monthly Magazine*, April 1860.

all of them, eventually let slip what they had found. As a result, by the time that Bronson and his friends returned to Willow Creek the following May, they were greeted by a host of excited gold seekers who had already scoured many of the creeks and gulches on the west side of Baldy Mountain. The Bronson men laid out five 200-foot claims on both sides of Willow Creek near their Discovery Tree. Unfortunately, even though they worked the claims for the rest of the summer, they only recovered fourteen ounces of gold.

A group of Ft. Union men calling themselves the Michigan Company found the first gold further up Moreno Valley in the gold-laden gravel of Michigan Gulch. Other prospectors followed their lead, among them, Pete Kinsinger, one of the original discoverers at Willow Creek. He and his associates located promising gold flats at the mouth of Grouse Gulch which they called the Spanish Bar.

By midsummer more than 130 claims had been recorded in the valley and more prospectors were on the way. With so many men entering the district, several of them met to organize the mining activity. They drafted a constitution that outlined the size of each placer and lode claim and how much work was necessary to keep them active for a year. Also, with the increase of traffic through Cimarron Canyon from Maxwell's ranch, crews worked all summer to improve the road for the prospectors.

The gold deposits discovered in the creeks and gulches of the Moreno Valley, known as placers, had eroded out of Baldy Mountain in ages past. The miners in the 1860s employed the standard technique of using water to separate gold from the gravel by first shoveling gravel into

*Prospectors swarmed
the Baldy area looking
for gold, using pans
and rockers to find
loose gold, and digging
tunnels into hard rock
to bring out ore.*
From *Harper's Monthly
Magazine*, April 1860.

long inclined boxes called sluices and then forcing water over it. The gold particles, being heavier than the gravel, collected behind crosswise wooden blocks or riffles and were retrieved by the miners when the gravel washed away. Often mercury or quicksilver was used at the bottom of the sluice to cling to and amalgamate with the smallest gold particles.

To meet the demand for water at the placers, crews began work in the early summer of 1867 constructing three ditches at the head of the valley to capture run-off water. At the same time several sawmills were erected to cut lumber for ditch flumes, sluice boxes, and miner's cabins.

So many men came to prospect the Moreno Valley that summer that John Moore, George Buck, and others organized a township for them on the west side of the valley opposite Baldy Mountain. They surveyed town lots for both businesses and residences with ample avenues in between. The town was named Elizabethtown in honor of Moore's daughter, and before the summer ended it boasted five mercantile stores that sold supplies to the miners.

As winter approached, mining operations gradually shut down because of freezing weather and the shortage of water for sluicing. Elizabethtown served as the off-season retreat for the miners while they waited out the cold. To alleviate boredom, the miners resorted to the recently erected May Flower Saloon, an establishment that served all sorts of refreshments and employed a number of females who catered to the various needs of the miners. Reports came in that winter that more than $100,000 in gold had come from the Moreno Valley placers during the summer, which created great anticipation for the forthcoming season.

In the spring, weekly stagecoach and mail service was established from Maxwell's ranch to E-town. By July 1st the coaches began to run daily. For eight dollars a passenger received a one way ticket to the placers transported in a modern Concord coach that was usually loaded with gold dust for the return trip.

Two hotels opened in E-town during the 1868 season. The Moreno Hotel opened its doors first and celebrated the event with a lavish banquet. The eighty-plus guests who attended were served on fine china dishes. It was reported that enthusiastic revelers found numerous reasons to toast each other with champagne during the course of the evening. The E-town Hotel was the next to open. It also offered sumptuous meals to miners along with overnight accommodations. The two-story structure was built by Henry Lambert who claimed that before he headed west he cooked for General U.S. Grant at Vicksburg and President Lincoln at the White House during the Civil War.

In addition several stores opened which offered supplies, whiskey, and groceries to the miners. Sugar could be purchased at "40 cents a pound, coffee at 45 cents to 65 cents, hams at 35 cents, flour at 10 dollars a 100 pounds, bacon at 45 cents a pound and vinegar at one dollar a pint." Added to these establishments were two restaurants, a drug store, a gambling house, and a billiard hall that boasted only one table. Town lots in Elizabethtown sold for between $800 and $1,200. By the end of June twenty stores and saloons graced the town.

Melvin W. Mills, a young lawyer, described life in the miners' camp.

> The predominating law seemed rather more a sort of six-shooter law rather than anything else, though there were several lawyers, such as they were, pretending to practice but actually living by mining, gam-

Early photo of Elizabethtown with Baldy Mountain in the background.
Courtesy of Elizabethtown Museum.

bling, or some other way. There were several halls of a hundred or two feet depth, generally having a liquor bar in front for the saloon part, then in the rear were the gambling tables with the dance hall. These halls usually ran all day or at least all night. The male dancer compensated for his privilege of dancing by going up to the bar after each dance, where he and his partner partook of the luxuries kept there for the occasion.

The frequent visits produced a lot of conviviality, stirring up the wilder men, who always had hung to their belts this six-shooter law and very often declared the law unto themselves, playing at such amusements as shooting out the lights in the halls and then shooting quite promiscuously until a stampede resulted, when the crowds would tumble over one another in the dark amid the screams of the more refined sex, until all would be quiet again, except for the groans of the wounded who lay dying after the commotion. Little was said next morning except that the shooter 'got his man' last night.

The mining activity in the Moreno Valley did not escape the attention of Lucien Maxwell who claimed the area as part of his land grant. He was cordial to the miners, mainly because they purchased so many supplies at his store in Cimarron. Over the first winter he sent Colonel J.D. Henderson to the valley to lease claims to the prospectors. A miner was allowed a 500-square foot claim and could lease it from one to ten years for $1 a month. By the end of February he had leased 1,280 claims.

Excitement also built over the winter in the valley when the legislature of New Mexico Territory formed a new county in January which encompassed the land grant. The new county was named in honor of the Vice President-elect Schuyler Colfax, and Elizabethtown was chosen as the first seat of Colfax County.

The miners again worked the placers furiously when the 1869 season started. In May they produced almost 250 pounds of gold valued at $18 to $22 an ounce. One group working in Willow Creek used a six-inch hose to spray water under high pressure over the gravel, which substantially accelerated the process of separating the gold. Called hydraulicking, this technology was highly efficient as long as enough water was available. But since run-off from the mountains decreased by mid-summer, most of the placers in the valley had to be shut down.

Several projects were instigated and engineered to increase the amount of water available for use at the placers. Foremost among them was the "Big Ditch" promoted by Lucien Maxwell, Captain Nicho-

Hydraulic mining near Elizabethtown, New Mexico.

Courtesy of Philmont Scout Ranch.

las Davis, and others. They organized the Moreno Water and Milling Company in May with the intention of bringing water from the Red River Valley into the Moreno Valley by engineering a series of ditches and flumes. The project took over a year to complete and employed four hundred men to construct the wooden flumes needed to carry water over the many gulches and valleys. One flume was 2,800 feet long and was trestled eighty feet over its canyon floor. Once completed, the Big Ditch was forty-one miles long, contained more than three miles of aqueducts and flumes, and cost $200,000. It was described as "an engineering feat of the first magnitude."

The first water from the Big Ditch reached Moreno Valley at Humbug Gulch above Elizabethtown in July 1869. Disappointingly, because of leaks and breaks that developed along the line, it only delivered 100 inches of water instead of the seven hundred it was designed to furnish.

While miners worked the Moreno Valley, prospectors were also active on the east side of Baldy Mountain along Ute Creek. Matthew Lynch, Tim Foley, and Robert Doherty were the first to discover deposits in the creek in May 1867. Encouraged by what they found, they marked the spot and discontinued work until the following spring. When they returned they agreed that a large deposit of lode gold was probably buried inside the mountain. Consequently, they again panned the creek until they no longer recovered flakes. They then began searching the ridge between Ute Creek and the Ponil River until they discovered a thirty-foot depression of decomposing quartz which sparkled with gold flecks. Further investigation revealed three veins that were three feet wide and six feet apart. The deposit was so rich that the gold was visible even to the naked eye.

Lynch immediately contacted Lucien Maxwell who, with V.S. Shelby and Colonel Edward Bergman, filed location papers for a lode mine on Aztec Ridge where they hoped to follow the gold-bearing veins. They called their mine the Aztec, and the first ore samples that Maxwell sent to the Denver Mint came back assayed at $19,445 per ton in gold and $189 in silver.

To process the ore from the Aztec mine, Maxwell and Lynch purchased a fifteen stamp mill in Chicago. Each stamp weighed 425 pounds and pounded the ore thirty-three times a minute to crush the ore to fine powder. The powder was then conveyed into "a sluice box through which ran a rapid stream of water. Most of the gold, being heavier than the associated powder, settled at the bottom of the sluice. What did not was caught by a layer of mercury in the bottom of a second sluice."

Colonel Bergman superintended the mine and oversaw five miners. In the first six days of operation, the miners extracted and milled 120 ounces of gold valued at $2,640. The mine and mill ran intermittently over the winter, but in May it began producing $15,000 a week from a recently discovered pocket of ore. By the time the year ended, the Aztec showed a gross profit of $180,000. Meanwhile, prospectors continued to work the placers along Ute Creek. In July one lucky miner found a nugget worth $40 in the bottom of his sluice box.

Maxwell was a seven-twelfths owner of the Aztec. The profits derived from the mine along with proceeds he received from sawmills along Ute Creek and the Moreno Valley, as well as the lease and sale of mining claims and lots at Elizabethtown and Cimarron, added substantially to his financial coffers. But with the increased income came countless frustrations caused by dealing with the miners along with the many farmers and stockmen who resided on the grant. This became so troublesome that Maxwell actively sought a buyer for his property in early 1869. After long negotiations, Lucien and Luz Maxwell agreed on May 26th to give three Colorado men "an option to purchase all of the estate except their Cimarron home ranch of one thousand acres." During the following January, Maxwell agreed to a selling price of $1,350,000.

The Colorado men represented a group of English capitalists who wanted the property, but who, under territorial laws, were prohibited from owning American real estate. The Englishmen organized the Maxwell Land Grant and Railway Company and planned to continue mining operations along with leasing and selling portions of the grant for mining, farming, ranching, and lumbering.

Unfortunately, mining profits began to fall off because the placer deposits in Moreno Valley and Ute Creek had mostly played out by 1870. Hydraulic mining was constantly plagued by the lack of sufficient water to work the area, as well as by frustrating geologic faults and eroded features that made it difficult to follow the veins and locate deposits. In addition, the company ran into increasing opposition from miners to leasing their claims. The lack of nearby railroad transportation impeded processing of large amounts of ore.

By the end of the 1870 season, most of the accessible rich deposits had been worked. Consequently, the majority of miners in the Moreno Valley slowly left in search of better fields in other parts of the West. Illustrative of the departure, Henry Lambert closed his hotel in Elizabethtown in 1872 and moved to Cimarron where he opened the St. James Hotel, still an important landmark in the town. That same year the Territorial Legislature also moved the county seat to the site of Maxwell's ranch in Cimarron.

The early "boom" years for mining on Baldy Mountain had passed, but throughout the next several decades the "boom" and "bust" cycle would repeat itself. They say the Baldy mines ultimately yielded several million dollars worth of gold over their lifetime. The Aztec Mine alone produced over $4,000,000, but that does not account for operational costs which reduced the net profit. After the early "boom" years, mining in the area never proved to be quite as profitable as predicted. Nonetheless, the excitement on Baldy Mountain was a powerful force that forever shaped the Cimarron country.

Unusual Wedding at the Aztec Mill

Reverend Thomas Harwood arrived in New Mexico in 1869 to begin what would become a life-long ministry as a preacher and educator in that territory. His account of the secret marriage of Captain Keyes to Virginia Maxwell in 1870 is made all the more interesting because Lucien Maxwell was the cantankerous father of the bride.

For marriages, baptisms, burials, etc., Methodist preachers are not allowed to charge anything, but most of the people said, "We don't do business in that way," and insisted that I must accept at least as a present what they gave.

March 30, in Cimarron, Captain A.S.B. Keyes and Señorita Virginia Maxwell were united in marriage by me. Present were Isaiah Rinehardt and wife. The marriage took place up in the third story of the large stone grist mill belonging to Mr. Maxwell. The room was strangely decorated with buffalo hides nicely tanned. Also bear, deer, mountain lion skins, nicely tanned, with other strange ornaments too numerous to mention.

As the marriage of Captain Keyes and Miss Maxwell produced no little excitement, it deserves a fuller notice. It endangered the preacher's life, subjected him to many threats of violence of different kinds. It was

From *History of New Mexico Spanish and English Missions of the Methodist Episcopal Church, Vol 1* by Thomas Harwood, 1908: 84-91,100,106-110, adapted by Steve Lewis

*Reverend Thomas Harwood,
Methodist circuit rider who
performed the wedding.*

the first wedding and the last one that he has ever performed contrary to the wishes of the parents, but this was a special case. He understood it well and conscientiously performed the ceremony, notwithstanding the fact that he knew the parents would object. The lady was of age, well educated and well informed, and had resolved to break away from the long-established customs of the country of the parents selecting a husband or wife for their children. They wanted her to marry a wealthy Mexican in the Rio Grande. She said she hardly knew the man, did not love him nor ever could, and she would never marry him.

She said she did love Captain Keyes, and she said: "I shall marry him, and you, Mr. Harwood, are the only one who can help me out." She had written me a nice, carefully worded letter, informing me that she had fully made up her mind to marry Captain Keyes, but her parents were so much opposed to it that the marriage would have to be done in secret and kept secret until they could get away. She also invited me on my next visit to Cimarron to call at their house and to call for her.

I did so, and found her to be a well-informed, self-possessed and accomplished young lady, a graduate of a school in St. Louis. She seemed to know exactly what she wanted to do. She had her plans well matured and all I had to do was to simply say I would perform the marriage ceremony and do it. I advised her to inform her parents what she intended to do just as she had informed me, and in a little while they would likely consent to their marriage. But she said: "They must not know of it. If father knew of it, he would be so angry he would tear down every house about the place if he could not prevent it in any other way. No, they must not know it."

But I asked, "Could you not get a justice of the peace to perform the ceremony?" To that she emphatically replied, "No, the only justice of the peace near us is my uncle, and he would inform my parents at once. They must not know it until we get away."

"But Miss Maxwell, do you not see where it would place me? You and Captain Keyes will be gone and I will be left, and I am here as a missionary, a Protestant minister, and I must not place myself where your parents and all your friends will despise the ground upon which I walk. And if your father will be so angry that he will tear down all the houses in the place when he hears about your marriage, will he not tear me to pieces for performing the ceremony?"

At this she seemed not to know what to say, but in a moment she seemed to recover and replied, "My father is not a vindictive man, and as you live quite a distance away, he will be over it by the time he sees you." I could not but admire the noble sentiments of this young lady. I said to myself, "This is one of the noble qualities of Protestantism. It is progress. It is independence. It is surely as it ought to be."

With these reflections I found myself yielding to her wishes...I went on my next appointments at Red River and Vermejo, and returned on March 30th. She had it all planned. No army general could have planned for a battle more wisely than she had planned for this marriage. She had made a confidante of Mrs. Rinehardt, a good Methodist and the miller's wife. It was an Indian ration day. There would be hundreds of Apaches at the mill to draw rations of meat and flour. "Mr. Keyes is their agent," said Miss Maxwell, "and will be there to issue rations to the Indians. Mrs. Rinehardt and I will go down to the mill at 4 p.m. You must go down a little before that, and go up into the third story of the mill. Mrs. Rinehardt and I will go down to the mill, then go up to the third story where I shall expect to find you and Mr. Keyes.

When I go home," said Miss Virginia, "mother will ask where I have been, and I will answer that I went to the Mill to see the Indians and get weighed. Guess how much I weigh, mother?" It all turned out just that way. The mother never mistrusted.

I found the third story of the big stone mill fixed up very nicely. The room had been swept and carpeted with different kinds of robes, and it was a real cozy place for a marriage ceremony. I pronounced them "man and wife" in regular Methodist style. It was several weeks before

Lucien Maxwell's three-story grist mill on Indian ration day about 1870. Virginia could easily keep watch for her father from the upper east-facing windows with a view of the Maxwell mansion.

they got off to his Eastern appointment, and the marriage was never found out until they were on the stage near Trinidad, out of the territory. When they met the south-bound stage, the Captain handed the stage conductor a copy of the marriage certificate with my name to it and told him to give it to Mr. and Mrs. Maxwell at Cimarron. From Trinidad, Mr. and Mrs. Keyes sent me a line informing me that they had gone and I at once informed Mr. and Mrs. Maxwell that I had performed the ceremony.

On April 26th Father Dyer was again in Cimarron. On the way to the home of L.B. Maxwell, where the famous wedding of his daughter, Virginia, had taken place, I told Father Dyer about the marriage. He was afraid that Maxwell would give me trouble, or some of those who were hanging around him hoping to get a little of his money when he sold the grant.

I wrote a real affectionate letter to Mr. and Mrs. Maxwell, expressing much sorrow for them, explaining why I performed the ceremony, and expressing hope that it was all right and that they and other friends of theirs would take a considerate view of the matter and become reconciled to it. They never made any reply, but other letters came, some from friends and some from foes, saying that it would not be safe for me to come up to Cimarron for some time.

A man told me afterwards that he rode up to Mr. Maxwell's store in the dark, and Maxwell thinking it was the parson, snatched him off his horse. One man was going to duck me in the water; another was going to black-snake me, etc. There was so much of it I got tired of it, and I had some serious thoughts. I said to myself, I have been a soldier under Grant and Sherman and Howard and Logan and Rusk; shall I now cringe like a cur before such fellows as these who are scraping and bowing to a rich man with the hope that they will get a few crumbs from his sale of the grant? I said, "No, the Lord helping me, I will go up to Elizabethtown and fill my next Sunday appointment."

I had not, up to this time, carried a pistol...but in this case, I borrowed a Colt's revolver and buckled it on the horn of the saddle and started. The first day out I had no trouble, but began to find that I had more friends than I thought I had. Nearly all the Americans said, "You did right." One prominent American said it was the bravest thing that has ever been done in this country. The next day before I reached Cimarron, I concluded I would not risk going through town, but take a trail that was quite a cut-off as to distance, but was a rough trail.

The next day as I rode up into Elizabethtown. Passing a saloon, a man came to the door and said, "There comes that Methodist preacher" with a terrible oath, at which several came to the door. I took hold of the pistol, but didn't draw it from the sheathe. No one made any further remark...One man said, "I think Mr. Maxwell will challenge you to fight a duel with him. If he does, what will you do?" I replied, "If Mr. Maxwell challenges me to fight a duel with him, I shall very respectfully decline. If he calls me a coward, I shall tell him that it is a brave man who can say 'No' against public sentiment."

Virginia Maxwell Keyes, later in life with two of her granddaughters.
Courtesy of Arthur Johnson Memorial Library.

I preached with unusual liberty on wrong-doing in general and lack of moral principle in particular as witnessed in some men who are almost ready to bow down and worship a man if he has money. "If you let a man influence and control you because he has gold, is it the man or his gold that controls you? Suppose the man's wealth should consist in a thousand Texas steers instead of gold; who then controls you, the man himself or his long-horned steers? I think the steers."

I have never regretted the celebration of the above marriage, especially when I have watched their career, that they have lived a happy and honored life, raised a large family and given their children a good education, most of whom are now married, settled down in life, and doing well.

Mining in the
Cimarroncito District

At the time gold was discovered near Baldy Mountain in 1866, prospectors swarmed the western portion of the Maxwell Land Grant searching for new mining claims. A solitary man with a gold pan could locate pockets of free or loose gold and work the claim himself. Virtually all the streams in the Cimarron country were prospected to some degree, and enough gold was detected on Cimarroncito Creek to warrant further exploration. By 1868 several placer mining claims had been filed in that area.

The process of prospecting began by locating loose gold in the gravel along a stream. The miner logically assumed that a gold deposit was higher up in the mountains, and that over time the gold had been washed downhill by the action of weathering and erosion. In order to locate the source of the gold, he would move upstream, noting the amount of gold in the gravel. When he reached a point where the loose gold diminished, he assumed that the source was somewhere nearby. From that point he would begin searching for an outcropping on both sides of the stream, from the bottom of the canyon to the top.

The Prospectors, Frederic Remington.
Courtesy of Library of Congress Photographs Division.

By Steve Lewis

In his popular 1895 mining manual, *Prospecting for Gold and Silver,* Professor Arthur Lakes at the Colorado School of Mines documented the methods used for decades by prospectors in the Rocky Mountains.

> A vein outcropping on the surface becomes oxidized and crumbles by action of the atmosphere, rain, etc. Pieces break off and fall downhill. "Float" is a rusty, spongy mass of rock showing iron and often some copper stains. He tries to trace this "float" to its home in the ledge whence it came. Of one thing he is certain—the "float" must have rolled down and not uphill. If he finds his "float" at the mouth of a canyon, he walks up that water course, noticing whether the "float" decreases or increases, and also noting any peculiar rocky pebbles such as porphyry which he might recognize again further up, giving him a hint as to whence the stream derived its material.
>
> He notices if the "float" fragments suddenly cease at a certain point. At that point he hunts for the ledge on either side of the canyon. If the "float" is scattered over the lower zone of the hill, and no "float" is found above that zone, he will hunt for his ledge at the top of that zone. If the "float" is all over the hill, he assumes the ledge is on the top. The character of quartz veins and of their enclosing rocks in the immediate vicinity decides the character of the gravels derived from them, hence sometimes a peculiar pebble may be traced up to the peculiar rock whence it came, and the gold vein be found near it.

Once he found the likely source of the gold, the prospector collected samples of the rock. Often he would crush the rock and wash it in his gold pan to see how much loose gold it contained. If the samples looked promising, he would take them to an assayer to determine their value. In order to stake a claim to his discovery, the prospector would

Prospector panning for gold at the edge of a mountain stream.

Courtesy of Library of Congress Photographs Division.

measure a rectangle 1500 feet by 600 feet around the outcropping. At each corner he would build a pile of stones or drive a stake, noting his name, the date, and a description of his claim. At the nearest recorder's office he would file the paperwork and pay a small fee to document his right to the minerals on that site.

During the early years of prospecting in the Baldy area, hundreds of enterprising men flocked to the region. One of these young men was Thomas Knott, raised in Ohio but recently discharged from service in the 2nd Missouri Cavalry ("Merrill's Horse") after seeing fierce fighting during the Civil War. By 1870 Knott had taken up residence in Elizabethtown, where he was a laborer in the gold fields around Baldy Mountain. As Professor Lakes declared, "The best education is in the mines themselves," and

Thomas Knott, about 1904.
Courtesy of Bruce Black Collection.

this is exactly the kind of on-the-job training that Thomas Knott acquired. He gained practical experience working the ground, observing expert prospectors, and learning to identify mineral deposits that would yield valuable ore.

The Black Horse mining claims were discovered in 1871 just a mile southeast of Baldy's summit, and Thomas Knott's name would be associated with those mines throughout their early history. Some of the ore samples were valued as high as $100 per ton, but the average was between $5 and $10 per ton. Over a period of two decades, the Black Horse group would yield around $27,000 in gold. By prospecting widely in the region during those years, Knott found additional outcroppings similar to those near Baldy. The new prospects were located across the ridge south of Cimarron Canyon at the headwaters of Cimarroncito Creek.

In a letter to his father in Cincinnati, Knott wrote, "I have been in the mountains all this summer, seldom coming into the settlements unless obliged to. I have been quite successful in making some new discoveries and finding gold in paying quantities. I have also erected some simple machinery on one of my mines and find that it will pay very well." After registering the Gray Eagle and Red Jacket claims he reported, "I have just called a meeting of the Gray Eagle Mining Company of which I am the head and principal discoverer. There are five parties now interested, and our property is well worth at the lowest figures one hundred or one hundred & fifty thousand dollars."

Knott contacted a London agent to promote the mines, and he received word "that he would have no trouble in disposing of our property for the amt of sixty thousand dollars, but I will not agree to sell for that amt as long as there is a show for to get nearer the amounts that our property is worth." He asked his father to contact capitalists in Cincinnati who might be interested in purchasing the mines. "Now if you are acquainted with any of those men, I think that there is a good show for the old man and his boy to make a big stake." Knott promised to send gold and silver ore samples for his father to exhibit for potential investors.

During the years immediately following Lucien Maxwell's sale of his land grant to British investors, there were many arguments over the ownership of mining properties. In this letter to his father, Thomas Knott hinted about an issue with the deed to his properties when he said, "As far as the title to our property is concerned, I can almost assure you that it is good as the dispute between us and the Maxwell Land Grant & Railway Co is about settled."

By 1880 Thomas Knott was established in Cimarron and rooming with another Ohioan named Charles Welles. They were both in their early thirties, and that year they registered claims for the Thunder and Contention mines at what became known as the Cimarroncito mining district. The following year it was reported that a group of investors from Pennsylvania and Illinois purchased the claims for $15,000.

Interior of the Contention Mine.

Courtesy of Larry McLaughlin, *PhilmontMovie.com*

Stock speculation in western gold properties had become commonplace by that time. For years, eastern investors had seen the shipments of gold dust and bullion from the mines of Colorado and New Mexico. Capitalists began buying and selling mine properties, and creating paper corporations to accumulate investments.

In his 1880 guidebook, *Colorado: Its Gold and Silver Mines*, Frank Fossett described how "mines—good, bad, and indifferent— were bought up in rapid succession. The war inaugurated a speculative era in which men acquired wealth with a rapidity they had never before dreamed possible." Shortly after the end of the Civil War the New York Board of Mining Stocks was established to facilitate the organization of companies and the purchase of mines, which were often valued at much more than their actual worth. Fossett explains:

> As time passed the excitement increased, and so anxious were people to possess a mine or some mining stock that the quantity of properties fell short of demand. Agents were sent out to hunt up and purchase mining claims. It is evident they were not very particular as to the value thereof, so long as they could show evidence of a transaction of some kind. Yet when a company was formed, these Eastern manipulators stocked what they paid the miner but a few thousand dollars for at a hundred times the original prices...It was the age of greenbacks, and as these promises of the government were steadily depreciating, it was feared they would eventually become worthless. This was one inducement for investing in anything that promised to give gold instead.

The April 1885 edition of *Harper's New Monthly Magazine* carried the following piece explaining how these New Mexico gold properties were capitalized and brought to market for eager investors.

> The brilliant showing made by New Mexico at the Denver Mining Exhibition in the summer of 1882 opened the eyes of outside people to the resources of the territory...The professional prospector, when he hits upon a promising claim, does not wait to realize a large sum upon it, but sells out for a few thousand dollars. Single great mines, or mines of great promise, have thus passed through a number of hands before their final capitalization at a million or so in the Eastern stock market. The man in New Mexico is poor indeed who does not carry a mine stock in his pocket.

Stamp mill for crushing gold-bearing rock.
Courtesy of Library of Congress Photographs Division.

In November 1883 Thomas Knott incorporated the Four Creeks Mining Company. This was not intended as a short-term, speculative venture because the company still had an active listing in the 1897 *Mine & Metallurgical Record* more than a decade later. The Four Creeks company owned the Black Horse group in the Baldy area, and in the early 1890s it purchased five claims in the Cimarroncito district. The most important properties in that area were still the Thunder and Contention mines, originally prospected by Knott and Welles. Thomas Knott knew first-hand of the potential for gold-bearing ore in the Cimarroncito district, and he was hoping to profit from it yet again. Near the turn of the century, however, he sold out and left the Cimarron country, eventually making his way to Los Angeles and San Francisco.

It was probably about this time when another young man from the East arrived in the Cimarron country. Born in Pennsylvania, two years before and eight miles south of the Gettysburg battlefield, Charles G. Cypher was a twenty year-old Huntington Township shopkeeper in 1880. Ten years later he was a resident of Cimarron and a full-fledged "quartz miner." He may not have known it at the time, but Cimarron would be his home for the next forty years.

In April 1900 the Consolidated Verde Mining and Milling Company purchased the Cimarroncito claims. They began to develop the Thunder mine under the direction of mining engineer Robert Selden Rose, a recent graduate of the Michigan College of Mines. Forty year-old Charles Cypher was employed as the site manager for mining operations, probably due to his recent experience in that mining district.

It is a complicated challenge to make an existing mine productive. Because most of the readily accessible gold had already been extracted, what remained was ore with more complex chemical structures which required more sophisticated processing. The nearest mineral processing plants were located hundreds of miles to the north, so high transportation costs would severely limit the profits to be made from such mines. This was nowhere more true than for the Cimarroncito mining district at the turn of the twentieth century.

By 1904 the Consolidated Verde Company found itself in financial difficulties. One speculator wrote to the *United States Investor* journal asking, "What is the condition of the Consolidated Verde Mining and Milling Company of Colfax County, New Mexico?" The journal replied,

> We understand that this is a corporation composed of Michigan parties altogether. Until about a year ago they were operating copper prospects in Colfax county. Correspondents write us that they have

Log cabin built along Cimarroncito Creek around 1900.
Courtesy of Larry McLaughlin, *PhilmontMovie.com*

found claims against the company still unsettled, and that the incorporators seem to be in a wrangle among themselves.

On February 6, 1904, the journal reported:

> The mines owned by this company are now inactive. More than 1,000 feet of development work was done on this property in tunnels and crosscuts, and some fine roads and buildings were also constructed. No mill was ever built. Some shipments of sample ore showed good values, but the pay ore was insufficient to warrant further expenditures. Fully $100,000 was spent in developing this property. The reason for the suspension of work is understood to be a failure to find large bodies of pay ore, and a lack of funds for further development.

The company was restructured as the Cimarron Mountain Mining Company, but by 1905 the speculative aspects of mine development had claimed yet another corporate victim.

What this mining district needed was a railroad to provide lower-cost bulk transportation for its ore, and in 1906 the St. Louis, Rocky Mountain, and Pacific Railway arrived in Cimarron. It is not a coincidence that in November 1908 the Cimarroncito mining claims were sold to the newly organized St. Louis and Cimarron Mining Company, composed of a group of the railroad's investors. Charles Cypher was retained as the mine's manager.

This venture was short-lived, however. Even with available railroad transportation, the total cost of extracting gold and other precious metals from the Cimarroncito mines still exceeded the profits. As one mining expert explained in the February 1917 edition of *Colorado School of Mines Magazine*, "It should be understood that an investment in

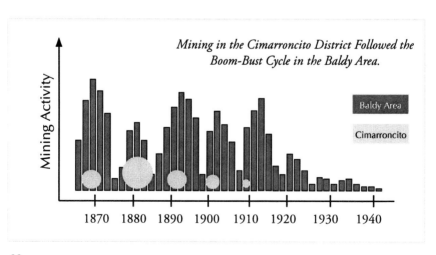

Mining in the Cimarroncito District Followed the Boom-Bust Cycle in the Baldy Area.

mining stocks is in most cases purely a speculation, not an investment. Most mines are so highly capitalized that the proceeds from their operation must be enormous in order for the investor to receive dividends."

Mining in the Cimarroncito district closely followed the boom and bust cycle of the Baldy district. When interest was rekindled in the Baldy mines, there was usually a corresponding interest in other nearby properties. Although exact figures are not available, gold production in the Cimarroncito district never reached even a fraction of what was taken from the Baldy area. While active mining continued periodically on Baldy until the 1940s, large-scale mining had ceased along the Cimarroncito around 1910.

Even after the mines were closed, Charles Cypher remained in the area. By 1910 he had married Bertha Brooke Benson in Albuquerque, and they made their home in Cimarron. In 1920 Cypher was listed as a grocery store salesman, and in 1930 at the age of 70 he is identified as a farm laborer. Early in the dust bowl years, Charles and Bertha Cypher moved to Springfield, Missouri, in order to care for Bertha's aging mother. Charles Cypher lived to be 89 years of age, passing away in Springfield on August 30, 1949.

Today the Thunder and Contention mines are still visited by hundreds of Boy Scouts who hike Cimarroncito canyon every year to camp in the area now known as "Cypher's Mine" at Philmont Scout Ranch. Young people can tour the Contention Mine and several of the original buildings in the camp. They sometimes scavenge the huge tailings pile of the Thunder Mine looking for samples of pyrite or semiprecious garnet stones. The sound of water and gravel swirling in metal gold

Scouts prospecting for gold on Cimarroncito Creek, Philmont Scout Ranch.

Courtesy of Larry McLaughlin, *PhilmontMovie.com*

pans continues to echo from the canyon walls, which would bring a rugged smile to Thomas Knott, Charles Cypher, and all those who have explored this beautiful canyon in bygone days.

Race for First Railroad into New Mexico

The first railroad into New Mexico entered the state at the northeastern corner of the Cimarron country, and from there it was built through the eastern plains of Colfax County. The contest to be the first railroad into the territory involved at least two Mexican land grants, three rival railroad companies, and four strong personalities who led the way. In the years prior to the Civil War there was an intense flurry of activity building railroad lines throughout the eastern states. Young men who gained experience in railroad building during that time would later use their skills to extend the railroads throughout the western states.

One of these young men was Cyrus K. Holliday, born in 1826 near Carlisle, Pennsylvania. By the time he was thirty he had earned a modest fortune building a railroad in his home state. The lure of the western frontier brought him to Kansas Territory in 1854. He became acquainted with Governor Charles Robinson, leader of the free state faction, and together they moved further west to find a good site for a permanent state capital. They purchased land on the banks of the Kansas River about twenty miles west of Lawrence, and here they established the Topeka Town Company, with Cyrus Holliday as the first president. By 1859 Holliday had a measure passed in the territorial legislature, with the consent of Congress, which made Topeka the territorial capital.

By Steve Lewis

Cyrus K. Holliday
Courtesy of Robinson Library.

As a man of some means, Holliday was interested in land speculation and town building on the new frontier, but as a railroad man he was deeply interested in building a rail line across the prairies. From the moment he entered Kansas he began to dream of building a railroad over the route of the old Santa Fe Trail. Railroad schemes were popular and commonplace in those days, but most of the chartered companies came to nothing. Many were organized on paper with millions of dollars in capital stock, but with absolutely no cash, no assets, and no offices. It was an age of overconfidence and speculative enterprise.

Holliday partnered with leaders in Atchison, Kansas, some fifty miles to the northeast, who wanted a rail connection with the new capital. Interestingly, Holliday had already written the entire charter for his "Atchison and Topeka Railroad Company," leaving only a few blank lines to fill in with the names of the incorporators from both towns. Toward the end of the legislative session Holliday and L.C. Challiss of Atchison, who were friends and members of the territorial legislature, introduced the charter to the council and it passed the following day. On the last day of the session, February 11, 1859, the governor returned the bill with his approval, and the Atchison, Topeka, and Santa Fe Railroad was born.

William Jackson Palmer
Courtesy of Denver Public Library Western
History Collection: Z-310.

About this time another young man, William J. Palmer, was also gaining railroad experience in the East. His uncle had sent him to study the coal mines and coal-burning locomotives in England and France. In 1857 he became private secretary to the president of the Pennsylvania Railroad, and two years later he was sent west to determine whether that railroad should build from Pittsburgh to St. Louis or to Chicago. The Civil War postponed Palmer's career as a railroad man, but he rose to the rank of brigadier general and earned a stellar reputation as the leader of the Fifteenth Pennsylvania Cavalry.

During the war years Cyrus Holliday was also busy laying a foundation for future railroad development across the plains. Before the war, Congress could not agree on legislation granting public lands and financial support for a transcontinental railroad. Northern politicians wanted the line built on a northern route, while southern politicians argued for a southern route. During the Civil War years Holliday wrote a bill which would make railroad construction possible, and he sent it to the US Senate in his own handwriting. It was introduced by Kansas Senator Samuel Pomeroy, where it quietly passed both Houses and received President Lincoln's signature on March 3, 1863.

This important bill was innocently titled, "An Act for a grant of lands to the State of Kansas, in alternate sections to aid in the construction of certain railroads and telegraphs in said state." It was general in character so any railroad company could appeal to it for assistance, but it specifically provided for "a railroad from the City of Atchison via Topeka, the capital of said state, in the direction of Fort Union and Santa Fe, New Mexico." Every alternate section of land for ten sections in width on each side of the roadbed was to be given to the railroad whenever twenty consecutive miles of track had been completed. One seemingly insignificant provision declared, "If any of said roads and branches is not completed within ten years from the passage of this act, no further sale shall be made, and the lands unsold shall revert to the United States." This deadline was to shape the destiny of the land grant railroads.

At the end of the Civil War, General William Jackson Palmer determined to focus his railroad-building efforts in the West. He envisioned how a railroad could turn seemingly worthless prairies and mountains into high-priced real estate. A decade earlier he had seen for himself on his travels through Europe that wealthy investors were eager to put their money into land speculation as new territory was opened for settlement and exploitation.

Palmer's first step toward his dream was to join the Kansas Pacific Railroad, a subsidiary of the Union Pacific. The original charter of the Kansas Pacific was to build a branch from Kansas City to Omaha, where it would join the main line of the Union Pacific. However, the directors soon decided to head for California on a southern route through New Mexico. In June 1867 the officers in St. Louis sent General Palmer to survey a number of southern routes and to recommend the best line to the Pacific coast. Meanwhile, in that same year Cyrus Holliday was pushing a local bond issue to provide $250,000 in county funds to begin construction of his railroad near Topeka, but he was unable to secure financing until late the following year.

Meanwhile, General Palmer led his survey party across Raton Pass and into New Mexico. It is obvious from his writings that Palmer was well-acquainted with the Cimarron country, as can be seen in his "Report of Surveys Across the Continent in 1867-68 for a Route Extending the Kansas Pacific Railway to the Pacific Ocean at San Francisco and San Diego." He provided detailed measurements for exact routes, roadbed grading, total rise and fall, character of the work, and resources available along the way.

Of the eight routes surveyed by his teams, General Palmer recommended the Raton Pass route. "The Raton Mountain Route is perhaps the best timbered of all the routes...Near the head of the Purgatoire, above Trinidad, and adjoining the Spanish Peaks, there is a large extent

ACROSS THE CONTINENT ON THE KANSAS PACIFIC RAILROAD

The Raton Mountains, Line of Southern Colorado and New Mexico.

1867 railroad survey photo from the top of Raton Pass looking south into the Cimarron country.
Courtesy of Boston Public Library.

of fine pine timber. From there to Fort Union the line is sufficiently close to the foothills of the Rocky Mountains on the west to obtain all that is needed."

He also commented on the extensive coal deposits in the Cimarron country: "In the Raton Mountain, and on both sides of it, were as many as twenty exposures of coal in at least a dozen different veins, the best of which was found in the cañons of the Vermejo and its branches, about 20 miles from the line, where were two beds of ten feet thickness, each admirably situated for cheap mining, and of great purity. This coal, which is bituminous, is hauled in wagons 70 miles for the use of the Government, for blacksmithing purposes at Fort Union. Apparently it is as good as the Westmoreland coal of Pennsylvania."

Water was extremely important for powering the steam locomotives, and Palmer reported, "From the Raton Mountains to the Pecos River, there is an abundance of good and permanent water in the frequent branches of the Cimarron, Canadian, and Pecos rivers, which the line crosses not far from where they emerge, sweet and copious, from the cañons of the Rocky Mountains." He also commented on the climate of the Cimarron country: "The route throughout is singularly favored in the matter of climate. The people of the eastern half of our continent have scarcely a conception of the physical pleasure of mere existence in the pure air and fine weather of this elevated southern plateau. For healthfulness, it is conceded to have no superior."

It was here that Palmer must first have observed the commercial prospects for the Maxwell Land Grant area. He wrote,

> From here to the Rio Grande is a good grazing country all the way, the vicinity of the Raton Mountains and the Cimarron Cañons being unsurpassed in the United States. No attention is required for stock in the winter. Even the summit of the Rocky Mountains, where the line crosses it, is covered with good grass. Throughout this entire country cattle, sheep, and mules can be raised so abundantly and so cheaply that the road will enjoy an immense business from their transportation, and that of wool and hides. The country is rich and beautiful, and contains a number of ranches. It is exceedingly healthy, and although the land requires to be irrigated, this is very conveniently and cheaply done in consequence of the abundance of mountain creeks. I counted five of these, with valleys averaging three-quarters of a mile in width, and enclosed between long, low spurs of the Raton Mountains...I saw a few fields of wheat and other crops, and very large herds of cattle and sheep.

General Palmer completed his survey, published his report in 1868, and recommended that the Kansas Pacific extend its line to California over Raton Pass. In the wake of the Civil War, however, Congress would not approve additional land grants to help railroad promoters, so Palmer's recommendations were shelved. Instead, he was assigned to build the Kansas Pacific's line into Denver. While in Colorado, Palmer

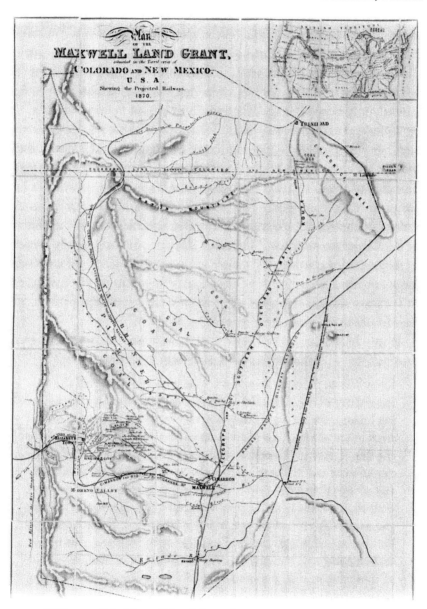

1870 map of the Maxwell Land Grant showing proposed railroad routes.
Courtesy of Palace of the Governors Photo Archives (NMHM/DCA).

decided to start his own railroad company which would use narrow gauge tracks to navigate the rugged Rocky Mountains. He envisioned his Denver & Rio Grande as a unique north-to-south line which would travel over Raton Pass through New Mexico and on toward Texas and Old Mexico.

Palmer's main difficulty was financing his new enterprise, since the government's policy of giving public land to the railroads had come to an end. He must appeal to Eastern and European investors, and because of his time in the Cimarron country he knew how to do just that. He was acquainted with William Gilpin, who had been the first governor of Colorado, and he knew that Gilpin acquired the Sangre de Cristo Land Grant in 1864 for about $40,000. Gilpin had sold half the grant to an Englishman, and they split the grant into Trinchera Estate on the north and Costilla Estate on the south. In total the grant contained 1,038,195 acres which covered the area between Colorado's Blanca Peak and the Rio Costilla near Taos, New Mexico.

From firsthand experience during his surveys Palmer knew that the Maxwell Land Grant was even more extensive, containing 1,714,746 acres between Colorado's Culebra Peak through the Raton Mountains into New Mexico almost as far as the Sweetwater River. General Palmer calculated that land which cost the owners only a few cents per acre would have its value multiplied many times by simply building a railroad into the area.

In the spring of 1870 Palmer learned that three Colorado land speculators were considering the purchase of the Maxwell Grant, primarily because they heard the D&RG railroad planned to build over Raton Pass into New Mexico. Palmer agreed to build the railroad if the land owners would finance the effort by purchasing bonds. Through a series of financial transactions the Maxwell Grant came to be owned by Colorado and then English investors—who promptly made General William J. Palmer the president of the new Maxwell Land Grant and Railway Company in order to seal the deal. Palmer made a similar arrangement with the English owners of the Sangre de Cristo Grant by agreeing to build a branch line over La Veta Pass into the San Luis Valley.

Meanwhile in central Kansas, Cyrus Holliday's little railroad had only built across the 62-mile stretch between Topeka and Emporia by 1870. However, land sales and transportation earnings had been surprisingly large. This allowed the AT&SF to continue building another

75 miles the following year to Newton, which instantly became an important cattle trail destination for stockmen from northern Texas.

Since the AT&SF was a land grant railroad it was able to capitalize on federal government support. Due to the ten year time deadline which had been written into the legislation, the AT&SF only had until March 3, 1873, to complete the line or it would lose its land grant. It now had less than two years to build the remaining 332 miles to the Colorado state line. Economic conditions were trending downward at the time and lending rates were increasing, as were the costs for labor and building materials. The directors estimated that it would take $5,000,000 to complete the line, and they determined to move ahead without further delay by raising funds to finish the line before their time ran out.

In May 1872 work started from Newton, and grading was fairly easy because of the level country. Chief Engineer Albert A. Robinson made record time building the grade to Hutchinson by June 17th, to Great Bend by August 5th, to Larned by August 12th, to Dodge City by September 19th, and finally to the state line by December 28th. The 3,000,000 acre AT&SF land grant had been secured with two months to spare, and the gross earnings of this ambitious little railroad totaled $1,172,013 for the fiscal year ending March 31, 1873. Skeptical people began to think that Cyrus Holliday's grandiose dreams may not be so foolish after all.

Unfortunately, the devastating financial panic of 1873 cut off capital investment, which curtailed railroad construction for about two years. In 1875, however, the AT&SF was able to build its tracks into La Junta, Colorado. By March of the following year its tracks extended to the northwest into Pueblo, Colorado.

During this same time General Palmer's previous employer, the Kansas Pacific, had renewed its interest in a southern route. At the town of Kit Carson, Colorado, it began building a branch to the southwest and it too reached La Junta by 1875. Eventually the Kansas Pacific directors chose to abandon the southern line, however, because they did not believe the area had sufficient resources to turn a profit. They removed their tracks in 1878 and never again offered any competition for a southern route.

In the mean time, William Jackson Palmer built the Denver & Rio Grande south from Denver to the Pikes Peak area. He adopted a policy of establishing company towns along his route because he understood that a railroad would multiply land values wherever it went, and he wanted that profit to go to his own companies. Instead of building into the existing town of Colorado City, Palmer platted a new town to the east and called it Colorado Springs. As the D&RG continued southward it bypassed Pueblo, and Palmer established the town of South Pueblo where the station would be located.

By April 1876 the D&RG had built tracks to within five miles of Trinidad, Colorado. There it established another company town called El Moro, and it began to sell lots to merchants who wanted to locate near the train depot. Needless to say, this angered the residents of Trinidad, which had a long and important history on the old Santa Fe Trail.

General Palmer's objective from the very beginning was to build his railroad over Raton Pass into New Mexico, and he was close to achieving his goal. However, another equally determined character entered the scene as Palmer's rival for the Raton Pass route. In 1877 the directors of the AT&SF appointed William B. Strong as general manager, and he would be the man to fulfill Cyrus Holliday's vision for a railroad across the Santa Fe Trail.

In February 1878 William Strong received reluctant permission from the AT&SF president to start "preliminary surveys in the spring" through southern Colorado and into New Mexico. That was the opening Strong needed, and he immediately ordered Chief Engineer A.A. Robinson to Raton Pass, "to occupy and hold it." Although both railroads had surveyed the pass, neither had taken the required step of filing claims with the government. Therefore, the first company to begin construction would establish their right to the pass.

Palmer received word of the AT&SF's movements in

Train entering a deep cut on Raton Pass.
Courtesy of Raton Museum.

February and he also dispatched a team to the pass, led by D&RG's Chief Engineer, John A. McMurtrie. The story is told that McMurtrie and AT&SF engineer Robinson unknowingly traveled on the same train from Pueblo to El Moro, which was the closest existing station near the construction site. When the train arrived at the depot McMurtrie went to his hotel, while Robinson rode to the home of "Uncle Dick" Wootton who operated the toll road over the pass. Around eleven o'clock that night Robinson was told that D&RG grading crews would begin work on the pass the following morning.

Since there was no time to lose, Robinson and staff engineer William R. Morley hurried to Trinidad and recruited a group of men with picks, shovels, and a few teams of horses. The citizens of Trinidad were eager to help, since the D&RG had bypassed them in favor of El Moro. Robinson placed work crews at several strategic points along the road, and they were busy grading for the Santa Fe line by five o'clock in the morning. One of the workers was said to be old Dick Wootton himself, who began shoveling by lantern light near the north approach to what would become Raton Tunnel. Shortly after sunrise the D&RG crew arrived, only to find their rival in complete possession of the pass.

For a time the D&RG crew looked for alternate routes over the Raton divide, but none were practical and the directors eventually abandoned the idea of entering New Mexico there. They focused their attention to the west where the rich mining camps of Colorado presented a greater opportunity for revenue. By December 1878 the Atchison, Topeka, and Santa Fe railroad had reached New Mexico and its course was set for southern California—ironically, using the exact route that General William J. Palmer had surveyed in 1867.

Early in 1879 the tracks were laid past the abandoned stage station of Willow Springs, and a new railroad town was established called Raton. Further south the rails were extended to the popular Clifton House station where the company created another town, calling it Otero in honor of businessman Miguel A. Otero who would later become governor of the state. The Santa Fe Railroad continued south and built the new town of Springer in 1879, named in honor of prominent attorney Frank Springer. The south-bound rail line then passed beyond the Cimarron country, eventually reaching Santa Fe by a spur line in 1880. New Mexico now had its first railroad, and this would bring dramatic changes to the Cimarron country in the years to come.

Through Cimarron Canyon to the Gold Camps

Charles Monroe Chase was the editor of a Vermont newspaper who traveled through the Cimarron country in the early 1880s, periodically sending reports to his paper back east. He humorously identified himself as the *Editor* and his traveling companions as the *Governor* and the *Invalid* (S.M. Folsom, who complained of dyspepsia but ate like a horse). His cousin Manly M. Chase also accompanied him on this visit to the gold camps in the mountains west of Cimarron.

Elizabethtown, N.M., October, 1881.

I have gazed upon scenery today which would surprise an inhabitant of the White Mountains, not because of more grandeur, of higher mountains, etc., but because the arrangement, the programme of sights, is wholly different from anything east of this range of mountains.

At eleven o'clock this morning the Governor and Mr. Folsom in one team, and Mr. Chase and the Editor in another, left Cimarron for this place, one of the famous mining towns in New Mexico. Passing up the Cimarron canyon for a distance of ten miles brought us to a place where the two ranges of mountains apparently come together—in other words, where the prairie, which had crowded itself in between the mountains for a distance of ten miles was prevented from further trespass by the mountains coming together at the base. Here the steep sides

From "In Elizabethtown, New Mexico" by C.M. Chase, *The Editor's Run in New Mexico and Colorado*. Montpelier, Vermont: Argus and Patriot Book and Job Printing House, 1882: 57-62, adapted by Steve Lewis.

Wagon road through Cimarron Canyon.
Courtesy of Philmont Scout Ranch.

of the foothills stop short at the bottom, where the flat prairie begins and stretches out one, two, three, or more miles in width, and then up go the steep sides again, which form the opposite range of hills.

At the end of the prairie strip we entered the narrow pass between the hills, and found scenery grand beyond description. The steep hills rose up on both sides and in front of us, and it seemed all the time as if we had been dropped down from above into an immense cavity of Mother Earth, from which there was no escape, except on eagle's wings. The view in front was against the broad sides of the great mountains, and there seemed to be no possibility of further passage, except over the dizzy peaks. But the road twisted, zigzagged, wormed around the base of the different hills, and although we were gradually rising, scarcely a hill was encountered in the highway. There is no such mountain pass in the East.

In one place, for an eighth of a mile the wall of the mountains rose up to a height of 800 to 1,000 feet perpendicular. Passing this, the great mountains rose up on either side, with immense projecting rocks, seemingly just ready to drop out of position. Nothing but confidence in a fastening which has resisted the storms of ages beyond historical knowledge, gives the traveler in that narrow pass a feeling of safety. In many places columns of rocks rose up independently to a great height, resembling a village of huge fantastic steeples, some resting upon bases so narrow that a tumble might reasonably be expected at any moment. But they are all there, and bound to stay.

At three o'clock, having grown hungry with riding and gazing, we stopped at a clear stream in the mountain gorge, unharnessed and baited the horses, built a fire, made coffee, and prepared a good meal from the lunch box. New Mexico men eat half their meals out of doors. All the drives are over long distances, and the lunch box is a most important part of the outfit. We camped by a beautiful trout stream, and being prepared with hooks and lines, I improved the opportunity. What luck? Well, I didn't count them. I always begin with "No. 1" to count, and as I didn't catch that particular fish the enumeration was omitted.

After washing dishes and repacking, the journey was resumed. Having passed through ten miles of the finest mountain scenery out of doors, we emerged into a "park" as it is called. Seven miles further brought us to Elizabethtown.

Elizabethtown is 8,200 feet above the sea level, and 1,800 feet above Cimarron. If the reader will recall the fact that Mount Washington is only between 5,000 and 6,000 feet above the sea level, he will realize that the Editor is considerably nearer heaven at this present time than when perambulating the Passumpsic valley. Elizabethtown village is not quite on mountain tops, but it is at the end of a basin or park 10 by 30 miles in extent, formed very near the tops, with "Old Baldy" the prominent point in front of it. Baldy is 12,000 feet above the sea, 5,000 feet above its eastern base and about 4,000 feet above Elizabethtown at its western base. Timber ceases to grow in this country at an elevation of 11,000 feet, consequently 1,000 feet of the old mountain's

Empty streets in Elizabethtown, with Baldy Mountain in the background.

Courtesy of Library of Congress Photographs Division.

top is bare headed, and hence the name "Baldy." The old head is a landmark, a geography indicator for people far and near.

In 1867 a party of hunters discovered gold here, gave the alarm, and
in less than two years there was a population of 4,000 people packed
here in the mountains. It sprung up at once into a city of great expecta-
tions. A company was formed which dug a ditch 42 miles long, at an
expense of $200,000 and brought water from the Red river. This was
the only stream available for washing the gold out of the hills, and in
a short time it was discovered that it was not sufficient for a quarter
of the miners. The boom was in 1869-1870, and during those years
Elizabethtown was built. Five miles below, Virginia City was started—
where a dozen or fifteen houses went up in haste, and as hastily came
down the next year. We passed through it, but there was nothing there
to mark the former existence of a village except one slight depression in
the turf where some aspiring candidate for worldly wealth had impro-
vised a cellar. Not a post or a stick or a stone could we see in the once
hopeful Virginia City—nothing but prairie grass and stillness.

In 1871 houses began to disappear from Elizabethtown, and in a
year or two the village of 2,000 people and surroundings of 2,000 more
dwindled to as many hundred. An Irishman named Lynch managed
to secure possession of the water ditch for $12,000 and has continued
mining ever since. His worth is variously estimated from $50,000 to
$1,500,000. We visited his works, saw the operation of gulch mining,
and the Irishman who owns the mine, who talks and looks like any
other Irishman.

I asked one of the men to show us a specimen of the gold. He went
several rods down the ditch, took a shovel full of dirt from the bottom,
and in five minutes had washed away the earth leaving on the shovel
part of a spoonful of fine sand and yellow dust. "How much is that
worth?" I asked. After a close inspection he said, "About one dollar sir."
I told him I was a stranger in those parts and would like to take it away
as a specimen. "And faith," said he, "it is not mine to give. The boss is
very particular." He laid the shovel down carefully, and while he was
answering some foolish questions put by Folsom and the Governor, the
dust was blown away. If the reader will call at my office next month I
will show it to him.

There are several others mining in a small way in this locality, all
doing well, but no extravagant stories are told. The work pays well,
probably $5 to $10 a day for a man's work. The "pay streak" is found

several feet under the surface, which make a great amount of washing necessary to obtain a little gold. A large surface of the country has been washed off. A few years ago several parties made small fortunes in a short time, and with little water. These were in places where the gold was found for quite a distance near the surface.

Readers who saw the operation of washing away the Bagley hill in St. Johnsbury saw a perfect illustration of gulch mining. The hill is torn away by the force of a stream from a two inch pipe. A wooden sluiceway conducts the water and dirt down the incline plane as far as needed, while men are stationed along to pick out the stones. Blocks of wood are fitted into the sluiceway, and on these blocks quicksilver is poured, which stops the little particles of gold. After the operation of washing has continued a week or two, the nozzle man takes a rest while the stone pickers shovel the loose dirt from the sluiceway, remove the blocks, shovel up the deposit, wash away the dirt mixture, then the owner boxes his gold and the operation of washing is renewed.

When the Lynch mine was started the pay streak was but a few inches from the surface, the washing was easy, and the mine consequently paid splendidly. Now the mines have got so far back into the hill that the pay dirt is ten feet below the surface, and the profits are much less. Another process of mining consists of tunneling down to the pay streak, which is shoveled up, taken to the smelters, where it is assayed and sold by the ton, priced according to the assay. When the

Hydraulic mining operation.

Courtesy of Library of Congress Photographs Division.

precious metal is found in the rock, it is blasted, broken up, passed through crushers, and then under the stamp mill, after which the dust is washed from the metal.

Our hotel accommodations at Elizabethtown were first rate. The ground floor of the building contained two rooms, a kitchen in the rear, and a combination dining room, bar room, and post office in front. But the beds were good and the landlord, Mr. Story, an American, had a German wife who knew how to cook. Folsom was obliged to allude to the altitude as an excuse for his appetite. I can't make it seem as if that boy was ever troubled with dyspepsia or any other ailment, but he intimates that he is out here for his health.

It makes one lonesome to walk the streets of Elizabethtown. Although not an old place, it is deserted and instead of the crowded street or crowded houses, bars, gambling saloons, and hourly knock downs of a few years ago, a sort of graveyard stillness, deserted buildings, and a general tumble down appearance is everywhere observed. There is one store, part of another, a hotel, the tail end of a barber shop, the outside of a Catholic church, a barn, a good deal of broken glass, and other fragments of former prosperity left, but the vitality of village life has departed, no more to return, unless more water is brought from Red River or some large companies are formed to begin pounding up the quartz rock by machine.

There is vast wealth in the surrounding mountains and specimens of rich ore are found in numerous places. The little village lives on, hoping for the start of enterprises which she is sure will pay. Mining is her only hope of existence, and this hope is strengthened by the success of mining in various localities in these hills. All through the hills of Colorado and New Mexico rich leads have been found and are being worked. Men are growing rapidly rich, and villages are springing up everywhere. Evidently the mining business here has scarcely commenced, for there is no end to the wealth the hills contain.

Ranching on the Maxwell Land Grant

"The profits of stock raising in this western country are so great that should I tell the truth, it might be taken as an exaggeration."
Journalist C.M. Chase on a visit to Colfax County, NM, in 1881.

The Spanish colonists of New Mexico brought numerous domes-ticated animals to their original settlement on the Rio Grande in 1598. Foremost among them were sheep. As time progressed and settlement expanded, Spanish flocks multiplied so much that by the time the New Mexican province began trading with Americans over the Santa Fe Trail in the 1820s, sheep wool and blankets were the dom-inant trade items exported to the east.

The Spaniards also raised cattle both for beef and as draft animals, but their importance was secondary. On the other hand, once New Mexico became an American Territory after the Mexican War (1846-48), cattle slowly replaced sheep as the primary stock. Frontiersman Lucien Maxwell was the first American settler in New Mexico to graze cattle. In the spring of 1848 he received a herd of cattle at his Raya-do ranch on the Beaubien and Miranda Land Grant. The cattle were driven over the Santa Fe Trail from Bent's Fort on the Arkansas River. In spite of frequent Indian raids, Maxwell's herds prospered. Although some of the cattle were used for beef, most of them were traded to travelers on the Santa Fe Trail who stopped at the settlement requiring replacement oxen to pull their wagons.

By Stephen Zimmer

Maxwell moved his ranch headquarters north to the Cimarron River in 1857. There he increased his herds to meet the demands of settlers on the land grant as well as soldiers at nearby Forts Union and Bascom. In addition, he supplied beef to the Jicarilla Apache and Ute Indian agency that was established at his ranch in 1861.

After Maxwell left Rayado, that ranch came into possession of his brother-in-law, Jesus Abreu. Abreu's ranch was described by Private Ovando J. Hollister, who camped there with the First Colorado Volunteers in March 1862 as they were en route to fight Confederates at the Battle of Glorieta Pass during the Civil War. In his memoir of the expedition, *Boldy They Rode*, Hollister wrote that the ranch "is situated on a small creek in a beautiful valley, and is composed of a plaza surrounded by adobe walls eighteen inches thick and eight to ten feet high. Excepting in front the walls are double and far enough apart to furnish a convenient apartment, say 12 feet in width."

He continued by saying, "This plaza is winged by similar smaller courts, walled in by houses. Adobe corrals for stock, and outdoor ovens of the same materials, finish the picture. It was constructed with a view to defense against Indians who were extremely hostile here ten years ago. The present incumbent is well disposed and liberal, giving us one hundred sixty pounds of sugar and one hundred of coffee, besides accommodating several companies with house rooms."

Jesus Abreu brand and earmarks.
From 1884 Brand Book of Northern New Mexico Cattle Growers Assn.

Jesus Abreu grazed large herds of sheep and cattle. He also raised horses, both for saddle mounts and to pull wagons and farm equipment. Stock marked with Abreu's Pear brand were recognized as some of the best in New Mexico Territory.

In addition, Abreu constructed irrigation ditches on each side of the Rayado to water fields of corn, wheat, oats, and hay along with orchards of apple, pear, and peach trees. To tend the fields and livestock Abreu employed Mexican farmers and herders who worked on shares. In exchange for half of each year's crop the men were provided with secure homes on the ranch. The arrangement was likened to the feudal systems of old, with Don Jesus serving as a benevolent patron over his loyal farmers and herdsmen.

In 1866 Charles Goodnight drove cattle over a trail he pioneered from Texas to the Horsehead Crossing of the Pecos River and then north into New Mexico Territory. From there his trail intersected the Santa Fe Trail at Las Vegas and continued over Raton Pass into Colorado. Goodnight sold many of his cattle to the military at Ft. Sumner and to the Navajo Indians on their reservation at Bosque Redondo. He also traded cattle to Lucien Maxwell on the Cimarron.

In the spring of 1867 Manly M. Chase came to Maxwell's grant to settle on the Vermejo River. Two years later he traded a herd of range horses to Maxwell for 1,000 acres along the Ponil River northwest of Maxwell's ranch. In 1871 he moved there and began building the adobe house that still stands at present day Chase Ranch headquarters. He also constructed irrigation ditches to water the native hay along the canyon.

Soon other stockmen arrived to take advantage of the rich grasslands of the region. John B. Dawson of Texas bought 3,700 acres from Maxwell along the Vermejo in 1869. He was familiar with the country, having previously partnered with Goodnight on several herds destined for the goldfields of Colorado. By that time Maxwell had acquired ownership of the entire land grant from Beaubien and Miranda, and it became known as the Maxwell Grant. The following year he sold it to an English holding company incorporated under the name of the Maxwell Land Grant and Railway Company. They planned to lease or sell lands on the grant for ranching, farming, lumbering, and mining.

Henry M. Porter, who had operated a store at Elizabethtown in the goldfields of the Moreno Valley, was one of the first to buy grazing land from the Maxwell Company. In 1872 he bought 640 acres and later leased an additional 23,000 acres along the Cimarron River and Urraca Creek. By 1880 he grazed more than 1,500 head of his OX and HMP branded cattle over the range. That year he and D.A. Clouthier opened a store in Springer, a town recently established on the Santa Fe Railroad. Their mercantile soon became the largest of its kind in northeastern New Mexico and provided supplies for all of the area ranches, including some as far away as the Texas Panhandle. A visitor to Springer in 1881 reported that the Porter and Clouthier

Henry M. Porter brand.
From 1884 Brand Book of Northern New Mexico Cattle Growers Assn.

*Porter &
Clouthier Store
Advertisement.*

store did $60,000 worth of business the month previous to his arrival. He also stated that "a ranch man may not come often, but when he comes, he loads up $300 to $1,200 worth of goods and departs for headquarters. The store alluded to is about 150 feet long, and is full of everything used by man or beast, from a cambric needle to a four horse wagon."

In 1873 Manly Chase and John Dawson formed a partnership to graze 5,000 head of cattle on the Vermejo River. In addition, Dawson pastured 8,000 head at his home ranch farther up the Vermejo where he also irrigated 300 acres. They were among the few cattlemen who owned or leased land from the land grant company, while most others simply grazed cattle on the grant, treating it as if it were open range.

CHARLES SPRINGER.

P. O., CIMARRON, N. M.

RANGE—Cimarron and Uracca Rivers.

ADDITIONAL BRANDS.

Thoroughbred Stock, **CS** on right side.

Some stock branded **B BX** right hip and side.

HORSE BRAND, **CS** on right shoulder.

CS Ranch brand list.

From 1884 Brand Book of Northern
New Mexico Cattle Growers Assn.

Attorney Frank Springer arrived in Colfax County from Iowa in 1873 to become legal counsel for the Maxwell Company. He was hired by William Morley, manager of the company, who had been a close friend while the two were students at the State University of Iowa. Soon after arriving, Springer bought 18,000 acres of range land along the Cimarron River from the company. He later established a headquarters west of the confluence of the Cimarron River and Ponil Creek.

His brother, Charles, joined him 1878 and together they expanded their holdings and formed the Charles Springer Cattle Company. The brothers imported the first Hereford bulls into northern New Mexico in 1881, which were branded with the now famous CS brand.

In 1880 the Maxwell Land Grant Company president, Frank R. Sherwin, purchased and leased company grazing land south of Cimarron. Five years later he sold his holdings and transferred the leases to Francis Clutton, who formed the Urraca Ranch and began raising well-bred cattle.

The arrival of the Santa Fe railroad in New Mexico in 1879 precipitated an even greater development of cattle ranching in northeastern New Mexico by opening eastern markets to area stockmen. The numbers of cattle grazing in the region reflected the rail line's importance. While there were an estimated 200,000 sheep and 75,000 head of cattle grazing Colfax County in 1875, seven years later the number of cattle had increased to nearly 500,000. At the same time the price per head also increased. 1879 saw cattle selling for $7 per head, while two years later the price had jumped to $12.

Over the winter of 1883-84 area cattlemen banded together to promote their interests and prevent rustling by forming the Northern New Mexico Stock Growers' Association. Headquartered in Springer, the organization's first brand book listed 150 members. The primary purpose of the association was to prevent cattle rustling, which had become rampant all over New Mexico Territory.

The Stock Growers Association also imposed other rules on its members. For example, it resolved "that any man who shall turn out female neat cattle upon the range should place with them, at the time of turning loose, not less than four serviceable bulls of improved quality for every one hundred head of female which are two years old or upwards at that time." Thus, as a group, the cattlemen committed to improving the quality and value of their stock. They also agreed that "no member shall gather cattle on any range not his own without informing the ranchmen in the neighborhood of his intention and giving them fair opportunity to examine the cattle before driving them away."

Stephen W. Dorsey brand.
From 1884 Brand Book of Northern
New Mexico Cattle Growers Assn.

Among those drawn to northeastern New Mexico and its cattle range was Senator Stephen W. Dorsey from Arkansas. In 1880 he established the Palo Blanco Cattle Company at Chico Springs, which was northeast of Springer on open range east of the Maxwell Land Grant. Dorsey pursued a policy common to many cattlemen across the West by instructing his cowboys to file homestead claims at strategic watering points over the public domain. This allowed him to control almost four million acres for his Triangle Dot cattle, which numbered an estimated 45,000 head in 1883, while holding deed to only a small portion of the range.

In 1881 the Maxwell Land Grant Company entered the cattle business and stopped leasing its land to others for grazing. The company's officers formed the Maxwell Cattle Company and named Frank Sherwin, Frank Springer, and Henry M. Porter to the board of directors. Manly Chase was hired as general manager. For the foundation of its

herd, the company bought 11,000 head already grazing on the land grant from Lonny Horn. The cattle were branded with his Long H brand which became the company's primary brand. Soon thereafter, an additional 5,000 head were purchased. The Maxwell Cattle Company eventually ran more than 30,000 head of cattle across 600,000 acres of the eastern part of the grant.

Maxwell Cattle Company brand.
From 1884 Brand Book of Northern New Mexico Cattle Growers Assn.

A visitor to the Maxwell Land Grant in the summer of 1888 wrote at length about the company's cattle operation. Taken as a whole, the description reflects how cattle were handled on unfenced range throughout New Mexico Territory at the time.

> This grant appears to be a most excellent cattle range. The mountainous portion is especially adapted to the raising of cattle. It abounds in grama grass, which is a very nutritious feed, somewhat resembling the buffalo grass of Colorado, but much superior. The soil is of such nature that cattle may be herded year in and year out over the same range, without its deteriorating in the least, which is, I believe, exceptional, and must add greatly to the value of the property. This fall the Grant will have a herd of some 30,000 head. Suppose each animal requires twenty acres, which is a liberal estimate; in that case their herd will have to range over 600,000 acres. It requires twenty men to attend to these cattle during the summer months, while but

half that number are needed during the winter. These twenty men will be divided into two outfits of ten each, counting the foreman and the cook, who does the work about camp. As each cowboy has from five to eight horses, an outfit will have in the neighborhood of sixty. These are of course supplied by the company, but the cowboy must furnish his own saddle and bridle.

During the summer months, their work consists in herding the cattle, rounding them up, branding the calves and breaking in their saddle horses. In winter there is not so much to be done. The outfit then goes into a permanent camp, living in a cabin made of logs, having the interstices filled with stones, plastered together with mud. From this camp they circle round through the country, bringing in the weak and sickly cattle, which they fear might otherwise not survive the winter storms, feeding them hay and alfalfa until they have recovered.

Whenever a round-up is held, all the cattlemen of the neighborhood are notified when and where it will take place, thus giving them a chance to send one or two representatives from among their cowboys to look after their interests. The outfit that is going to hold the round-up moves its camp to the open canyon where it is to be held. They then spend several days in collecting all the cattle they can find for miles around into one herd.

When the cattle have been rounded-up a few men stand guard, while the rest proceed to cutting out. This consists in separating the different brands from the main brand, which is necessarily that of the outfit on whose range the round-up is being held. One now begins to appreciate why the neighboring cattlemen must send representatives. Mr. Littrell [Marion, cow foreman] told me that the grant company had three or four men at as many round-ups on the adjacent cattle ranges. It is during the winter that the cattle wander the farthest. When the bleak winds begin to blow from the north, the cattle are driven south, ten, twenty, or thirty miles, according to the strength and duration of the storm.

Next in order after the cutting out comes the branding of the calves. As they always stay by their mothers, it is an easy matter to know to whom they belong. A big fire is built and irons heated. The men lasso the calves round the neck, by a leg, or any other way, and come galloping up to the fire with the bellowing calf dragging on behind, sometimes on all fours, but quite as often on its back or side. No time is lost. One of the men appointed for this duty passes his hand along the rope until he reaches the calf's head; he then slips his other hand over its back, and taking hold of the skin half way down the side, throws it with a jerk on the ground. The hot branding iron is now applied, and perhaps an ear cut off, and the calf, branded with the mark of its owner, is permitted to return to mother cow, who had been watching the operation with great anxiety. After all the calves have been thus treated, the cowboys depart and the cattle are again left to themselves.

By 1887 it was estimated that 600 settlers grazed 65,000 head of cattle, 3,600 horses, 16,000 sheep, and 2,000 goats on the Maxwell Land Grant. Until 1890 the majority of the cattle in the region grazed on open range that required communal roundups to brand calves in the spring and ship saleable stock in the fall. Most individual ranchers or cattle companies only held title to the water sources used by their cattle. After 1890, when the Maxwell Cattle Company and others began to fence their land, the cattle grazed in fenced pastures.

In 1892, the Maxwell Land Grant Company discontinued operation of the cattle department because of losses due to bad winters, cattle rustling, and wolf depredations. That year the company tallied 5,000 fewer cows than the year before, and the number of cattle that were sold barely equaled the number of calves branded. Consequently, the cow herd was liquidated, most selling for approximately $15 per head.

Crow Creek cabin and Maxwell Cattle Company cowboys about 1885.

Eventually, the stockman who grazed cattle on the grant either purchased or rented their ranges from the company or moved off. For those who chose to leave, the company bought their cows for $15 per head with the calves thrown in, and bought the improvements or structures they had erected. As a result, by 1900 the company was able to offer its range land for sale or lease unencumbered.

One of the first buyers was Englishman Harold Wilson who ranched in southwestern New Mexico Territory along the Gila River. Wilson and his partner, Montague Stevens, ran cattle branded with a WS. The two encountered many problems ranching on unfenced range, the greatest being rustlers who stole great numbers of cattle from their herds.

As a result the two cattlemen began searching for another range that they could fence in order to secure their cattle. In 1899 their ranch manager, Captain William French, learned about the Maxwell Company lands and traveled to Cimarron to inspect them. Suitably impressed, he bought 125,000 acres situated between the Ponil and Vermejo Rivers and added an additional 30,000 acres the following year.

Demand for other Maxwell lands was high due to the company's promotional efforts in newspapers across the eastern United States and Europe. William Bartlett, a grain dealer from Chicago, responded to one of the company's ads in the fall of 1900 and inquired about ranch acreage as well as land suitable for hunting and fishing. After inspecting the Maxwell lands in 1901, Bartlett bought 220,000 acres centered in the area known as Vermejo Park. That mountainous country was priced at 30¢ an acre, while the parks and pastures sold for a little more than a dollar an acre.

By the first decades of the 20th century these two ranches, along with the CS, comprised most of the land grant. The transition to private ownership was nearly complete after Waite Phillips consolidated several land grant ranches to form Philmont Ranch in the 1920s. Today most of the Cimarron country is still used for grazing, and cowboys continue to ride the range taking care of cattle as their predecessors have for over one hundred and fifty years.

The Pacing Black Mustang of Antelope Springs

R ange historian J. Frank Dobie had a great affinity for horses, especially the wild horses or mustangs which roamed the American West. Among the stories he collected in his celebrated book, *The Mustangs*, were those devoted to the courage, endurance, and beauty of several white stallions and their exploits in avoiding capture by mustangers. In these legendary frontier accounts most of the stallions escaped because they possessed a pacing gait that enabled them to outdistance their would-be captors.

A similar story, which Dobie described as "beautiful and true to range men as well as their horses," was gathered by naturalist Ernest Thompson Seton. Seton was wolf hunting on the L Cross F Ranch in northeastern New Mexico in the fall of 1893 when he became familiar with a mustang stallion of exceptional qualities. The story he heard differed from Dobie's accounts because this stallion was shiny coal-black instead of white, although he too was a natural pacer and had "thin, clean legs and glossy flanks."

Seton's pacing mustang was first observed as a yearling by a number of cowpunchers who made plans to catch him. Before anyone actually made an attempt, however, the colt had turned three years old and had taken charge of nine "half-blooded" mares who wandered away from the ranch. Initial efforts to gather the gentle mares were unsuccessful due to the black stallion's skillful handling of them. Soon a consensus was reached that the only way to get back the valuable mares was to

From "The Pacing Black Stallion of Antelope Springs" by Stephen Zimmer, *Western Horseman*, October 1997: 106-108.

either catch or kill the pacer. In December 1893 Seton set out from headquarters with the L Cross F wagon. The ranch manager told him, "If you get a chance to draw a bead on that...mustang, don't fail to drop him in his tracks."

The pacer was soon sighted by one of the cowboys. Seton took his rifle and climbed a ridge, expecting to take a shot, but the magnificence of the horse stopped him. He later wrote that the stallion "heard some sound of our approach, and was not unsuspicious of danger. There he stood with head and tail erect, and nostrils wide, an image of horse perfection and beauty, as noble an animal as ever ranged the plains, and the mere notion of turning that magnificent creature into a mass of carrion was horrible."

As a result of this encounter, Seton threw open the breech of his rifle. The cowboy with him reached for the gun, but Seton turned the muzzle to the sky and it "accidentally" went off. It was Seton's only sighting of the stallion, but while in New Mexico he heard other stories of attempts to capture that swift horse. He recorded some of them in his book of animal stories, *Wild Animals I Have Known*, which appeared in 1898.

One of those accounts tells about Wild Jo Calone, the cowpuncher who gave the most serious consideration to capturing the stallion. Most of his associates thought he was crazy to waste good men, horses, and time on an animal that probably had no value. However, when the owner of the Triangle Bar Ranch, in the presence of witnesses, offered a thousand dollars to anyone who could deliver the stallion safely to a boxcar, Wild Jo decided it was time to make his move.

With an outfit of twenty saddle horses, a mess wagon, cook, and a partner, he planned to walk down the mustang and his band. The mustanger's idea was to follow the stallion horseback at a leisurely pace until the horse got used to a trailing rider. Then Calone planned to continue to pressure the horse and wear him down so much that he would have little time to eat and drink. The cowpuncher then hoped to rush in and rope the stallion.

When all was ready Wild Jo led his outfit to Antelope Springs, the favorite watering place of the pacer and his band. When Calone's outfit spotted the stallion, the horse took alarm and led his mares away at a high lope across a nearby mesa. Jo quickly followed, and as he came upon them he slowed his horse to a walk. They ran again. The cowboy cut their trail at a trot as they circled to the south, and caught up with them after several miles. He again walked quietly toward the horses. When they took flight, Jo rode back to the wagon and arranged with the cook to meet at a place that would intersect with the horses' circle.

Wild Jo trailed the horses until dark and then switched with his partner, Charley, who took after the band on a fresh horse. By now the herd was getting used to the company of a trailing horseman. The horses did not run as far as they had at first. Charley walked after them for a few hours in the dark, aided not only by a sure-footed mount, but also by a white mare in the band who was easily seen in the pale moonlight. Later Charley stopped, unsaddled, and lay down to sleep on his saddle blanket by his picketed horse.

At dawn Charley found the herd no more than half a mile away. They immediately bolted, moving westward. Charley soon saw the smoke of the outfit's camp, and when he reached it Wild Jo took over to trail the herd. This pattern was repeated for the next two days. The

Portrait of Ernest Thompson Seton, about 1906.

Seton's famous painting of the pacing mustang pursued by Wild Jo Calone.
Courtesy of Philmont Scout Ranch.

horses continued to move in a circle, destined eventually to bring them back to their favorite water. Although the horses progressively felt more at ease with their pursuers, the constant travel, even at a walk, was beginning to wear on them. The band began to suffer constant nervous tension from the day and night pursuit.

Whereas Jo's and Charley's horses ate grain twice a day, the mustangs had to graze on the run, instead of locating a good stand of grass and eating at their leisure. The stress also caused them to become unusually thirsty. Wild Jo allowed the wild band to drink as much and as often as they desired, knowing how a running horse filled with water would get stiff limbs and lose wind.

By the fifth day the herd had almost reached Antelope Springs. The mares began lagging, in spite of the black stallion's efforts to urge then on. Often they were no more than 100 yards ahead of the relentless, trailing horseman. Wild Jo's plan had been executed with only one hitch. Whereas the mares were done in, the pacer seemed to be as strong as when the chase began.

When they reached the springs, Jo kept the herd from water for a few hours and then let them drink their fill. He soon realized that he would probably not have to rope the mares, because he could easily separate them from the stallion and drive them back to the L Cross F corral. Jo directed his full attention to the pacer. For the final chase the cowboy caught his favorite and fastest mount, *Lightfoot*. Although she was of eastern blood, she had been raised on the plains and Jo was confident she had the bottom to catch the stallion.

Jo took after the stallion at a run. On discovering his pursuer, the mustang jerked up his head and started off at his usual swinging pace. Jo was a quarter of a mile behind, and using shouts and spurs, the cowboy urged the mare to lessen the stallion's lead. The mustang led Jo across a long, grassy stretch, still maintaining the same even gait. The cowboy was astonished that the distance was actually widening between them.

Then, suddenly, his mare went down, the victim of a badger hole. Jo went sprawling, but quickly jumped to his feet to remount. The courageous mare, however, had broken her right foreleg and Jo sadly put her down. As he carried his saddle back to camp, he could see the stallion striding off in the far distance.

All was not lost for Wild Jo and Charley, though. They claimed a sizable reward for the return of the L Cross F mares, but Jo never forgot the pacing black stallion of Antelope Springs.

Catskill: The Rise and Fall of a Logging Town

Today, the dense forests that cover the mountains of northern and western Colfax County are a rich haven for wildlife. Species as diverse as golden mantled chipmunks, black bears, long tail weasels, elk, mule deer, and turkey are frequently spotted by observant hunters or campers as they trek through the woods. Trees are largely viewed in terms of their aesthetic and ecological value as opposed to their economic worth.

But during frontier times, the great stands of Ponderosa pine and Douglas fir were an important economic resource that fueled the growth of a number of lively settlements which are but faint memories today. Trees equated to mine timbers and railroad ties, and as a result the cry of "Timber!" was frequently heard in the mountains at the turn of the 20th century.

Before any trees could be cut and sold, however, rail lines had to be built into the mountains in order to transport logs out. Lumber camps grew up at intervals along the tracks and at the end of them, the remains of which are slowly but inevitably passing back to the earth.

Catskill is a typical example. Located about ten miles northeast of Vermejo Park, the camp was founded in the summer of 1890 when the Denver and Fort Worth Railroad began laying sixteen miles of track to the site on the headwaters of the Canadian River. In a contract with the Maxwell Land Grant Company, officials of the railroad agreed to operate the line as long as the mills in the area could cut an aggregate

By Stephen Zimmer

McAlpine's sawmill, Catskill, New Mexico, 1893.
Courtesy of Palace of the Governors Photo Archives (NMHM/DCA), #14258.

of 20,000 board feet of timber a day. Eventually, contracts were written with several companies to take 25,000,000 feet annually.

Although the railroad contract required that the tracks reach Catskill by August, the first steam engine did not roll into the camp until September 26th due to rains, washouts, and labor shortages. Moreover, the line was not stable enough for heavy traffic until November, by which time the lumberjacks and mill men were in full pursuit of their work.

The town site was located on a slope full of big pines along the river, with a spectacular view of the Sangre de Cristo Mountains opposite from where the railroad entered the canyon. The name Catskill was suggested by railroad general manager C.F. Meek, and as a fledgling town it grew rapidly with the influx of lumbermen. A school was completed in early 1891 to accommodate twenty students. By May there were seventy-four children attending, and plans had been drawn up for an annex.

By the end of that summer there were several restaurants, saloons, two large mercantile buildings, a blacksmith shop, and a community water system. The Brett Hotel was a two-story frame building, and the Fuller House was a second hotel constructed for the overnight comfort of visitors to the growing town.

Numerous entertainments were provided for the lumbermen as diversions from their labors. People could enjoy horse racing every Saturday on their own local track. In addition, they listened to the Catskill

Cornet Band on Sundays at the dance pavilion where an eleven-piece ladies' band also occasionally performed. Baseball was an ever-popular attraction that saw the local Catskill nine pitted against teams from several nearby communities.

Typical of the lumber companies contracted to work out of Catskill in the 1890s was the Maxwell Timber Company headed by J.C. Osgood. The company was licensed to cut and manufacture hewn railroad ties, telegraph, telephone, electric, light, and other poles, mining ties and props, stockyard and fence posts, and cordwood from trees too small to scale.

Charcoal was another product made from trees harvested near Catskill. Two sets of massive brick beehive-shaped charcoal ovens dominated the camp, one group consisting of ten ovens, the other of fourteen. Each oven was almost thirty feet high and thirty feet in diameter, and even today they are all in a remarkable state of preservation.

Timber royalties paid to the Maxwell Land Grant Company from Catskill lumbermen reached more than $110,000 annually in 1893. But after the readily available stands of pine and fir were cut, royalties dropped to around $30,000 by the end of 1897. Many men were put out of work, and the resulting stress was declared as the cause for an unprecedented amount of drunkenness. In an effort to curb such behavior, the Maxwell Company donated several acres to the local

Charcoal ovens at Catskill, New Mexico.
Courtesy of Raton Museum.

Population of Catskill, New Mexico, in fancy dress, about 1893.
Courtesy of Raton Museum.

chapter of the Women's Christian Temperance Union for a church to combat the "evil of drink."

Other problems beset the camp, foremost of which was the deterioration of the rail line. By 1900 sections of it had become dangerous, and the Colorado Southern Railway Company, now the parent line, was reluctant to spend the money necessary to repair trestles and re-tie the roadbed for the small quantity of timber remaining. The decision to discontinue the line was made in late 1901, and the company pulled up its tracks the following January.

A few townsmen hung on for a time, but most of the lumbermen moved to camps on a new timber railroad that had begun running outside of Cimarron. Soon all had gone, and Catskill, with its giant charcoal ovens, was left to the deer, elk, and bear.

The Deep Tunnel Mine

Disregarding the learned and scientific ideas and taking the common and accepted theory, there must be far richer and better leads than ever have been taken out in the Baldy region…Where there is all this "smoke"…There is certain to be a great and hidden fire.

New Mexico Miner, 1898.

Mining activity along the slopes of Baldy Mountain resumed and gained momentum in the 1890s precipitated by efforts of the Maxwell Land Grant Company to generate income from gold deposits located on the estate. The Aztec Mine was reopened, as were hydraulicking efforts in the placers of Moreno Valley.

The most ambitious project was undertaken by the McIntyre brothers, William and Alexander, who incorporated the Gold and Copper Deep Tunnel Mining and Milling Company in the fall

Extra timbering at mine's entrance, with hard-rock tunnel in the distance.
Courtesy of Library of Congress
Photographs Division.

By Stephen Zimmer

of 1900. Their plan was simple—bore a tunnel completely through Baldy Mountain—and find the mother lode.

Work began the following spring when miners opened a tunnel into the mountain at the head of Big Nigger Gulch directly opposite Elizabethtown. The first season's work resulted in a completed tunnel 300 feet in length that had been driven in a northeasterly direction and eventually reached a depth of 1,800 feet. The men used hand drills to bore into the rock the first season, but they adopted power drills afterward to speed up the work.

After a year of operation the brothers found they could not continue without outside financing. They decided to offer stock in the company to fund further drilling. Each year one brother stayed in New Mexico to superintend operations while the other travelled east to interest investors in the project. Enough money was procured to enable the miners to continue their dogged tunneling, but alas, the mother lode they so desperately sought escaped them.

Work on the tunnel was suspended in 1908 only to begin anew two years later. By 1912 the brothers had raised and spent more than

Mine interior with miner using candles for illumination.
Courtesy of Denver Public Library Western History Collection: X-61061

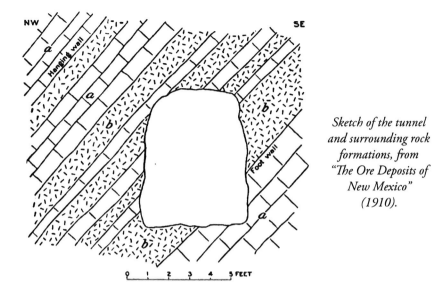

Sketch of the tunnel and surrounding rock formations, from "The Ore Deposits of New Mexico" (1910).

$200,000 on the project without ever being able to declare a dividend. Having run out of resources, the determined brothers were forced again to increase capitalization and sell additional stock. At the end of 1926 an additional $90,000 had been acquired for the company's coffers.

Unfortunately, William died in 1930, but his determined brother forged on without losing sight of their shared dream. In the spring of 1932 he directed some of the Deep Tunnel drillers to move to the other side of Baldy Mountain and set up operations at the head of South Ponil Creek. There they began tunneling in a southwesterly direction in hopes of intersecting the existing tunnel on the Moreno Valley side.

Four years later they celebrated the completion of the tunnel. Amazingly, the two tunnels connected with centers only one inch apart. The effort was an astonishing engineering achievement that was hailed throughout the West.

But to what effect? After thirty-six years of concerted effort and the expenditure of hundreds of thousands of dollars, not an ounce of gold was ever found. In the end the Deep Tunnel Mine was abandoned and slowly filled with water. The grand dream of the McIntyre brothers was never fulfilled, and the mother lode remains hidden beneath the rocky slopes of Baldy Mountain to this day.

Last of the Train Robbers: The Black Jack Gang

A long the walkway leading to the museum at Philmont Scout Ranch sits a large boulder with a face carved on it. Legend has it that the face is a likeness of the notorious train robber Black Jack Ketchum, who inhabited the Cimarron country in the late 1890s.

The rock originally stood at the entrance to Cimarron Canyon in the piñon-studded foothills west of town. A small wire corral made to hold horses had once stood behind it. Some local old timers claim that the spot was Black Jack's lookout, where he and his gang had an unobstructed view of the plains to the east. They also say that the face was carved by one of the gang members as a symbolic statement of Black Jack's vigilance in watching for pursuers.

Other local observers are equally emphatic that the carving was done by a Pinkerton detective who had been sent into the mountains west of Cimarron to discover the whereabouts of Black Jack's hideout. Since the rock was located on Philmont property, officials had the boulder moved from its original site to the museum in the late 1960s.

The Black Jack Ketchum in question was born in Texas with a given name of Thomas near the end of the Civil War.

Face on the Rock.
Courtesy of Philmont Scout Ranch.

From "Last of the Train Robbers: the Black Jack Gang" by Stephen Zimmer.
High Country, Summer, 1999:41-43.

He was the youngest of three brothers. The oldest, Berry, tried to ride herd on his rambunctious younger brothers Sam and Tom after their parents died. He had little success.

During their late teens Sam and Tom punched cows for a living, but they grew to love gambling and horse rustling just for fun. Robbing mercantile stores and post offices also occupied their leisure time. They were handsome men, both tall and physically strong. Sam was fair-skinned with blue eyes and red hair, while Tom was dark-skinned with dark eyes, hair, and mustache. He usually dressed in dark clothing, and it was later said that his sombre appearance is what led to the sobriquet of Black Jack, although the origin of the alias has not been satisfactorily resolved.

The brothers first came to New Mexico in the late 1880s, first to John Chisum's ranch on the Pecos River, then to the Dry Cimarron country northwest of Clayton. Contemporary observers said they headed west more to escape arrest warrants than to find new ranges to ride. The historical record is unclear when the brothers determined that robbing trains would be a satisfactory diversion and a suitable source of gambling stakes. By 1887 they had been joined by old friends from Texas, Will Carver and Dave Atkins. The group spent much of that summer in Cimarron, gambling and drinking at the St. James Hotel and other local saloons. It was reported that Tom, although a lover of the gambling table, rarely drank. However, he frequently displayed a streak of generosity by buying drinks for the house.

Supposedly during their stint in Cimarron the gang formulated the plan to rob their first train. Foreseeing a future necessity, they also es-

tablished a hideout in the upper reaches of Turkey Canyon northwest of town. They outfitted a cave with log barricades and a corral near a clear pool of water that was fed by a small stream.

About ten o'clock on the night of September 3, 1897, the quartet stopped and took possession of a passenger train south of Folsom, New Mexico. They were successful in opening a small safe and dynamiting a larger one. The explosion wrecked most of the express car, but they absconded

Thomas "Black Jack" Ketchum with a good part of the scattered money.

Their tracks led toward Cimarron, although they continued toward another hideout in southern Arizona.

Over the next two years they robbed several trains in southwestern New Mexico, and reports implicated Black Jack's gang as the perpetrators. Tom and Sam were also identified as the robbers of two West Texas trains held up in the spring of 1898.

A year later Sam Ketchum showed up again in Cimarron. He was joined by two new associates, G.W. Franks and William McGinnis, a.k.a. Elzy Lay, a former member of Butch Cassidy's Wild Bunch. Tom's whereabouts at the time were unknown, although it was later reported that his absence was due to a falling out between the brothers.

St. James Hotel (background), a favorite haunt of the Black Jack Gang.
Courtesy of Old Mill Museum.

While in Cimarron, the three hatched another plan to rob the train that ran through Folsom. On the evening of July 11, 1899, the trio stopped a Colorado and Southern train at almost the same spot they had two years before. They made away with several passengers' bundles and an undetermined amount of money, and again they headed for Cimarron.

A few days later they were seen riding into the mouth of Turkey Canyon, where they were followed on July 16 by a posse led by two deputy US marshals and a sheriff from Colorado. The lawmen tracked the train robbers into the upper reaches of the canyon, where they noticed the smoke of a campfire in the late afternoon. They spotted the three train robbers as they approached the camp.

After taking defensive positions, the lawmen opened fire. In the ensuing battle the sheriff was killed and several other posse members were wounded. Hostilities ceased when it began to rain. During the night the desperados made their escape, two suffering from bullet wounds.

Sam Ketchum, the most severely wounded, was apprehended at Henry Lambert's ranch on Ute Creek a few days later, and was eventually sent to the New Mexico Penitentiary in Santa Fe. He died there from complications of his wounds on July 24, 1899.

McGinnis was later captured and tried for the murder of the sheriff in the Turkey Canyon shoot out. He was convicted and sentenced to serve time in prison. After six years the governor of New Mexico commuted his sentence. Franks was never captured.

Some years later, Fred Lambert, the son of the owner of the St. James Hotel, met a man by the name of Pegleg Sullivan who had recently moved to Cimarron. After the men became acquainted, Sullivan divulged that he was, in fact, G.W. Franks of Black Jack's gang. He verified his identity by reminding Lambert how the two had once taken target practice behind the St. James when Fred was a teenager.

Black Jack's last train robbery attempt near Folsom, New Mexico.

John Norval Marchand illustration from *Munsey's Magazine*, February, 1902.

Sullivan—or Franks—was only in Cimarron for a short time, however, because he contracted a flu virus that caused his death. Lambert reported that the man had a great deal of money which he would liberally spend on the local townspeople.

A month after the shoot out in Turkey Canyon, Black Jack attempted a solo robbery of the same Colorado and Southern train south of Folsom. The holdup went awry, however, and Ketchum was seriously wounded in the arm by a shotgun blast from conductor Frank E. Harrington.

Black Jack staggered away, and the train continued on its route. The next day the desperado was captured without resistance by the Union County sheriff. Several days later his arm was amputated, and he was sent to the State Penitentiary in Santa Fe.

Ketchum's nefarious career ended when he was convicted for attempted train robbery in October of 1900, which was an offense punishable by hanging. Black Jack's day at the gallows came on April 26, 1901, in Clayton. Witnesses reported that he stoically walked to his place under the hangman's noose, evidently resigned to his fate. When the trap door was released, his weight caused his head to be severed from his body.

Like many western outlaws, Tom Ketchum became better known after his capture than during his active career. The contemporary newspaper accounts of the train holdups and murders did not identify the Ketchums by name. It was only after they were apprehended that their exploits came to light. They were the last of the outlaws who once infested much of the Wild West. As New Mexico was settled and the arm of the law spread across the land, their kind could not flourish.

Many still wonder what became of the gang's ill-gotten gain. Waiting for his hanging in a Clayton jail cell, Black Jack told newspaper reporters that his men never spent or gambled it all away. He even sent several treasure seekers on wild goose chases into isolated spots in Colfax County, Cochise County, Arizona, and West Texas where he said the gang had cached stolen money. This writer's hope is that someday a cowpuncher prowling a remote high country canyon west of Cimarron will find a stash of Black Jack's gold.

A Railroad for Cimarron

The promoters and stockholders had plans as ambitious as their company's name. Incorporated in 1905 as the St. Louis, Rocky Mountain, and Pacific Railway Company with a capital stock of $2,250,000, they intended to lay track from Raton to Cimarron, then westward to the goldfields of the Moreno Valley, and eventually to the Pacific coast by way of Taos.

But, alas, they got no further than Ute Park in the Cimarron Canyon before their capital ran out. Their achievement was nevertheless impressive for by opening markets to area farmers, ranchers, and mine operators they brought a new economic prosperity to Colfax County.

The railroad was a subsidiary of the St. Louis, Rocky Mountain, and Pacific Company which controlled over 500,000 acres of bituminous coal fields between Raton and Cimarron. They operated mines at Brilliant, Koehler, and Van Houten. The officers and directors of the company included Thomas Harlan, Henry Koehler, Hugo Koehler, and Max Koehler of St. Louis, as well as Frank and Charles Springer of the CS Cattle Company, and J. Van Houten, president of the Maxwell Land Grant Company. By establishing a rail line the company not only furthered its own interests, but it benefitted the endeavors of the entire region as well.

Construction on the line southwest out of Raton began in late 1905 under the direction of the Utah Construction Company of Ogden. Fourteen months later the line was completed to Ute Park, an under-

From "The St. Louis, Rocky Mountain & Pacific Railway" by Stephen Zimmer, *High Country*, Summer, 2003: 39-42.

St. Louis, Rocky Mountain & Pacific engine 101 steaming through Cimarron Canyon.
Courtesy of Old Mill Museum.

taking that required more than five hundred men and three hundred teams of horses to grade the roadbed. Although work progressed quickly on the relatively level land from Raton to Cimarron, the company's engineers encountered great difficulty extending the line westward due to the rugged terrain in Cimarron Canyon.

The SLRM&P also tended a line east from Raton to Des Moines, which gave it a connection with the Colorado and Southern Railway. This, coupled with a link to the Santa Fe system at Raton, ensured the railroad's access to lines running north, south, and east. Once completed the line was 105 miles long and boasted seven steam locomotives, 558 freight cars, and five passenger cars. All equipment carried the company's *Rocky Mountain Route* slogan that included a Native American swastika symbol centered in the design.

The first Rocky Mountain train destined for Cimarron left Raton on December 10, 1906. That day a large and enthusiastic crowd of ranchers, farmers, miners, and townspeople gathered in the little town to celebrate the locomotive's arrival. Blacksmiths' anvils were charged with gunpowder and exploded when the flag-draped train arrived pulling cars loaded with company dignitaries and well-wishers. The festive atmosphere continued throughout the day and presumably into the night as well.

Cimarron was designated as the site for the railroad's roundhouse and repair shops, which were completed in the spring of 1907. The shops were described by the *Cimarron News and Press* as being some of the most thoroughly equipped in the Southwest. Under the direction

Excursion by rail and community picnic in Ute Park, New Mexico.
Courtesy of Old Mill Museum.

of master mechanic J.W. Records, who was assisted by able machinists in each department, the shops were capable of turning out what the newspaper termed "all classes of railroad and repair work."

To stimulate passenger traffic on the line from Cimarron to Ute Park, the SLRM&P constructed a dance pavilion at Ute Park in the summer of 1908. An excursion train filled with celebrants traveling at special rates left Raton to inaugurate the opening of the facility on Sunday, June 14th. The highlight of the day's festivities was a baseball game between players from Van Houten and Cimarron. The *Cimarron Citizen* reported that the ball park had "not as yet been put in very good condition, but a fine flat field was chosen as the scene of the meeting between rival twirlers of horsehide and wielders of the bat, and one of the best games of ball witnessed in the county this season was the result."

Afterward, those assembled moved to the pavilion for an evening dance and orchestra music furnished by the railroad. Simultaneously, the pavilion's lunch counter "catered to the wants of the hungry crowd in a most efficient manner." The newspaper further reported that once Ute Park became better known to the summer pleasure and comfort seekers, the railroad planned to build an immense resort hotel and lay out ball, polo, and other grounds, an eventuality, at least at this writing, that has not yet come to pass."

After a number of years of operation, rumors began circulating among the county's populace that the Rocky Mountain Route might be incorporated into a larger rail system. Those suspicions were confirmed

Freight cars ready for loading at Cimarron station.
Courtesy of Old Mill Museum.

in 1913 when the Atchison, Topeka, and Santa Fe Railroad Company purchased the little rail line and renamed it the Rocky Mountain and Santa Fe Railway. Unfortunately for Cimarron, the Santa Fe decided to service all of the line's cars at its Raton shops and by early 1914 they dismantled the Cimarron roundhouse and moved it to Raton.

The Rocky Mountain continued hauling coal, cattle, and farm produce as before. Passenger traffic, however, remained light, although sightseers frequently availed themselves of the opportunity for a relaxing train ride up the narrow, rock-walled Cimarron Canyon to Ute Park. The experience was perhaps best described by railroad employee Edward Mahoney who recorded some of his early reflections in 1962.

> I usually contrived to be out on the open observation platform, going up the canyon from Cimarron, with my feet propped up on the brass railing. How I would like to relive one of those trips [with] no cares...relaxing, taking in the scenery, and inhaling the odors of pine, sage, and good locomotive coal smoke—listening to the engine working up the two-percent grade, hearing the flanges squeal on the tight curves, and enjoying the sight and sound of a rushing mountain stream which we crossed and recrossed many times.

The Santa Fe decided to abandon the Rocky Mountain Route in November 1942, due in part to the consolidation of its system during World War II. All that remains of the line today is the roadbed, which is easily distinguished in many places between Raton and Cimarron by the long-unused telegraph poles that paralleled it. Likewise, up Cimarron Canyon to Ute Park the roadbed can be discerned, minus the bridges where it frequently crossed the river.

Cimarron station, with east-bound train ready for departure.
Courtesy of Old Mill Museum.

Although short lived, the Swastika Line's impact was great on all whose lives it touched, and the modern traveler cannot help but wonder what it was like to ride on the old train and hear the shrill whistle and feel the awesome power of its locomotive as it steamed along in the old days of the Cimarron country.

St. Louis, Rocky Mountain & Pacific engine 103 and her crew.
Courtesy of Old Mill Museum.

The Fruit of the Land

When you think of the Cimarron country you might not envision a place where lush orchards and sweet produce can be grown. However, around the time of New Mexican statehood, promoters were fond of praising the orchards of the Cimarron country. In New Mexico's official publication for the Panama-California Exposition of 1915, for example, the writers claimed, "Colfax County apples lead the world in flavor and quality." The accompanying photographs depicted vast orchard groves full of trees laden with heavy, ripe fruit. This literature claimed that the horticultural conditions in the Cimarron country were perfect, and that "apples of many varieties are grown in wonderful perfection of color, form, size, and flavor."

Historians have called the late 19th century "the golden years of apple growing," and it was during this favorable time that the first orchards were planted by settlers in the Cimarron country. Manly M. Chase may have been the first to cultivate apple trees near the headquarters of his ranch in Ponil Canyon. Shortly after he acquired the property Chase began to cultivate the arable valley into gardens and orchards. In 1872 he ordered 250 fruit trees from Ohio, and they were delivered to him by freight wagon

Display of prize-winning Chase apples.

By Steve Lewis

across the Santa Fe Trail. Chase found that the young trees grew well and produced large amounts of high quality fruit. He was encouraged by this success and expanded his orchards until they became a model for fruit growers throughout the southwest. Chase exhibited his apples at the Chicago World's Fair in 1893, where he was awarded a gold medal. It was said that the Chase orchards produced almost 500,000 pounds of fruit each year. In 1910 Chase wrote that the fruit was of such high quality that his orchard only experienced one crop failure in 35 years of production. Manly Chase lived until 1915, and in his later years his greatest pleasure came from tending his precious fruit trees.

One of Chase's close friends and business partners was John B. Dawson, who also planted fruit trees during the early years of his settlement in the Cimarron country. Dawson developed his ranch property in Vermejo Canyon several miles northeast of Chase's Ranch, but growing conditions for apple trees were just as favorable there. In the *US Congressional Serial Set* for 1893, Dawson is listed as "one of the old timers of this region who now has over 40 acres planted containing about 6,500 trees." His orchard was comparable to that of Chase, as the booklet explains, "Mr. Manly M. Chase, his neighbor from the earliest days, is the owner of an orchard of equal size and containing about the same number of trees."

Apple pickers in the Chase Ranch orchard.
Courtesy of Old Mill Museum.

This 1893 Congressional publication also listed other fruit growers in the Cimarron country during that period. Special mention is given to "the immense establishment of M.W. Mills," as well as M.E. Dane's "most promising collection covering 20 acres" northwest of Maxwell Station. In the Rayado area south of Cimarron, Jesus G. Abreu also had "a large and flourishing orchard principally of apples" during this time.

In 1901 the report of the governor of New Mexico to the US Secretary of the Interior listed the Dawson, Chase, and Mills orchards as the most famous producers in New Mexico. Governor Miguel A. Otero stated at that time, "Fruit growing and the management of the crop have been brought to a business standard on these big fruit ranches that is not excelled anywhere in the West, and certainly not in the Rocky Mountain region." In his similar report of 1904, Governor Otero wrote that "the Springer, Mills, Dawson, Chase, and other large ranches are famous for their fruit and alfalfa crops and their beautiful mansions. Apples, peaches, pears, and plums are the leading orchard products."

As late as 1917, Ralph Emerson Twitchell, in his multi-volume work, *The Leading Facts of New Mexican History*, listed the following fruit growing areas: "Fine apple orchards are growing at various points in the country near Cimarron, Springer, French, Maxwell, Rayado, Raton, Dawson, and so far as is known may be grown anywhere. Pears, cherries, and plums also thrive."

At Rayado, Jesus Abreu had passed away in 1900, and by 1907 his sons attempted to formally develop their property by creating the Rayado Land and Irrigation Company. They planned to build a complex system of ditches and reservoirs to bring more land under cultivation, but inexperience and lack of funds resulted in their selling the family ranch to a group of Colorado speculators in 1911. The new owners formed the Rayado Colonization Company and subdivided the ranch to promote the sale of smaller farms to families who wanted a fresh start in the West. This scheme failed to attract enough buyers, however, and even though the Rayado orchards continued to produce fruit, they deteriorated and fell into disuse within a few years.

Just after the turn of the century, the town of Miami was established further east along the Rayado River. In 1907 the Farmer's Development Company purchased 10,000 acres in this area, and they immediately began an extensive irrigation project using the latest and most innovative techniques then available. The company proceeded cautiously and developed the property conservatively.

APPLE ORCHARD NEAR CIMARRON   APPLE ORCHARD NEAR MIAMI

In 1917 Twitchell reported,

> The company never indulged in the usual noisy methods of land
> companies, preferring rather to let the land and its settlers do the
> advertising. Irrigation construction has always been well ahead of the
> demands upon it and the company has kept its credit clean and has
> otherwise kept itself in a position to more than fulfill its obligations
> to settlers.

In contrast to the typical speculative enterprises of that time, their
conservative approach seems to have brought positive results. The Miami community was said to contain attractive homes with lawns and
flowers on tree-lined lanes, as well as having a local church and school.
Six hundred acres were devoted to apple orchards, and Twitchell explained that "the encircling foothills, the peculiar adaptability of the
sandy loam, the perfect soil drainage and air circulation have caused
experts to predict that Miami will soon be numbered with the famous
apple-producing districts of the West."

North of the Rayado another ranch would also become a thriving
fruit growing property. The area south of Cimarron between the Cimarroncito and Urraca Creeks had been farmed periodically by several
of its previous owners, but they used the property primarily for grazing cattle and horses, and for alfalfa production. In 1910 George H.
Webster, Jr., the ranch manager of the former owner, purchased the
Urraca Ranch and immediately began to develop the agricultural potential of the property. Before he planted a single tree, Webster spent
several years studying the soil quality, drainage, air circulation, water
supply, fruit varieties, packing methods, transportation facilities, and
market locations.

A display of award-winning Urraca Red apples.

In the foothills about four miles west of the orchard, Webster built a private reservoir that would provide sufficient water to irrigate 2,000 acres. In the fields below the reservoir he divided 400 acres into 40-acre plots, each with a wide gravel road around the perimeter to ensure adequate access for pickers and haulers. The plots were planted with apple trees laid out on a triangular system so that all of the trees would be at least 30 feet apart. It was estimated that there were 23,000 trees in Webster's orchard, and only the five best commercial varieties were selected for planting.

A box factory was established in Cimarron, as well as a packing house, and crates of fresh apples were hauled to local railroad lines where they were shipped to markets across the country. Apparently, Webster even considered building a railroad spur south from Cimarron to the orchards, but market conditions did not justify it. By 1915 New Mexico's official booklet for the Panama-California Exposition report-

Urraca Ranch apple orchards, about 1914.

ed, "Perhaps the largest individually owned commercial apple orchard in the State of New Mexico is that located on the Urraca Ranch at Cimarron in Colfax County. Net profit on this orchard was nearly $200 per acre last year." This was the property that Waite Phillips eventually purchased in 1922, and which formed the foundation for what would become the immense Philmont Ranch. Even today many of Webster's apple trees are still growing in the area around Philmont's headquarters.

During its heyday, the fruit growing industry in the Cimarron country produced large amounts of high quality fruit, and it was recognized internationally with prestigious awards. As with any commercial enterprise, market conditions would ultimately determine the fate of this industry. Other areas of the nation began to develop fruit growing properties to compete for this market, and today almost half the nation's apples are grown in the state of Washington. New Mexico is resilient, however, and it continues to adapt to market conditions. For example, it recently became the second largest producer of pecans in the nation, carrying on the spirit and tradition of its pioneer fruit growers from the Cimarron country.

Logging and Railroads
along the Ponil

The story of logging in the canyons of the Ponil country is part of the continuing saga of exploiting the natural resources of the Maxwell Land Grant. At the beginning of the twentieth century the Maxwell Company was in desperate need of cash to pay its debts, and the Dutch owners were reluctant to spend additional money to develop the grant's resources themselves. Company president Frank Springer began to look for outside investors who would pay leases to develop the property or who would purchase it outright.

One of the grant's most promising resources was the coal-rich land on the northern part of the property. For several years the Colorado Fuel & Iron Company, and its founder John C. Osgood, had been eyeing the coal lands on the Colorado portion of the Maxwell Land Grant. CF&I was already the largest coal producer in the American West, and in 1901 Osgood purchased the Colorado side of the grant for a reported $800,000.

This was around the same time that Frank Springer found a group of St. Louis investors willing to lease the other coal properties south of the Colorado border, and they planned to build a railway from Raton to Cimarron. This sudden economic expansion on the grant created an immediate demand for railroad ties and mine timbers.

For quite some time Thomas Schomburg, the operations superintendent for the Maxwell Company, had been involved in exploiting the vast timber resources on the grant. Through the previous decade

---

By Steve Lewis

the revenue from timber royalties had been one of the most consistent sources of income for the company. In 1887 grant trustee Harry Whigham reported, for example, "The principal revenue from the estate for the past year was derived from royalty on timber," which he set at $2.50 per thousand feet. Even though some of the grant's timber had already been cleared by this time, the region around the Ponil canyons remained a very rich logging area.

Thomas Schomburg had been in close contact with J.C. Osgood, and in March 1901 the Maxwell Company gave Osgood a contract for all of its timber for a period of twenty years. The only condition was that Osgood build a railway from his Colorado properties southwest into Ponil Park. It was at this time that Schomburg left the Maxwell Company to take over management of Osgood's newly incorporated Rocky Mountain Timber Company. Osgood agreed to issue Schomburg forty percent of the company's stock in consideration for his proxies and services.

By 1902, however, Osgood began facing serious cash flow problems and he turned for help to George Jay Gould, the principal stockholder of the Denver & Rio Grande Railroad. Gould brought in John D. Rockefeller who helped engineer a corporate takeover of CF&I in 1903. By 1904 John C. Osgood, the self-made founder of the company, had lost control of CF&I and was forced out. As a result, Osgood was unable to build the logging railroad into Ponil Park, and the Maxwell Land Grant Company cancelled his timber contract in 1906.

Meanwhile, Thomas Schomburg had not been idle. He diligently studied the timber supply and estimated that the company could expect a profit of $3 per thousand feet even after paying royalties, and that the timber would not be exhausted for at least twenty years. Schomburg organized the Continental Tie and Lumber Company to negotiate a contract with the Maxwell Company that would replace Osgood's cancelled agreement.

Since the new contract also required the construction of a railroad to Ponil Park, Schomburg incorporated the Cimarron and Northwestern Railway as a subsidiary of his Continental Tie and Lumber Company. By the end of 1906 the St. Louis, Rocky Mountain, and Pacific Railroad had reached Cimarron, and Schomburg proposed to build his new rail line northwest from Cimarron into the logging area. Corporate documents filed on January 21, 1907, clearly show the purpose of the Cimarron and Northwestern Railroad.

Cimarron & Northwestern locomotive #1—a light engine called a "teakettle."
Courtesy of Denver Public Library Western History Collection: OP-6006.

The principal incorporator was T.A. Schomburg, president of the Continental Tie and Lumber Company, which purchased the standing timber on lands of the Maxwell Land Grant Company. The carrier is virtually a plant facility for the transportation of the lumber products of the Continental Tie and Lumber Company. To supply the mills and bring out lumber is the sole reason for the road's existence. When the timber is gone, the Continental Tie and Lumber Company, having no interest in the cut-over lands, intends to close the road and take up the rails.

The canyons of the Ponil country contained tens of thousands of acres of rich timber, especially virgin stands of Ponderosa pine and Douglas fir. At that time there was still a high demand for railroad ties, mine timbers, and planed lumber for building. Schomburg and his chief railroad engineer, A.G. Allen, immediately surveyed the route and began construction on the line in February 1907. By the end of that year they had built twenty-two miles of track, including sixty-seven bridges, between Cimarron and Ponil Park. On January 6, 1908, the Cimarron & Northwestern Railroad was operational.

With the transportation infrastructure in place, swarms of independent logging crews fanned out across the vast timber property. Each crew consisted of a few men with axes, hand saws, and teams of draft animals. Each man had a specific role. The undercutter chose the trees, and he would cut a notch on the trunk which indicated the best direction for the tree to fall. Two sawyers followed him and they would fell that tree while the undercutter chose the next tree. An axman followed

the sawyers to remove the limbs after the tree was down. He would also measure large trees into appropriate lengths for hauling, and the sawyers would return to cut the logs at his marks.

Often a single crew could cut 100 or more trees a day, depending on the size of the timber. An experienced axman would also cut a narrow road so the logs could be hauled out to the main loading area near the railroad line. Teams of draft animals would drag the bucked logs along these roads, and the man in charge of this operation was called the skidder. If the rail line was too distant then the timber was loaded onto heavy wagons to be hauled over a larger road to the main line.

Logging crews typically worked for themselves and were paid by the piece. They often lived in remote areas near their job sites so they could quickly begin work after sunrise and continue working into the evening. The hours were long, the work was difficult, and the accommodations were very primitive. Sometimes whole families lived and worked together, but more often the crews consisted of unmarried men. Sanitary conditions were poor, and the men would frequently wear the same clothes for an entire season.

In the Ponil country, clearcutting was the most economical way to exploit the timber resources. This method involved cutting every tree that the sawmill could use, and since this area contained large, old-growth timber, nearly all the trees were felled. The crews would usually harvest the best trees, leaving the low value ones that were rotten, diseased, or deformed. This practice is called "high grading" and it can negatively effect the genetic make-up of a forest over time because only the weakest trees survive to reproduce.

Since most trees were topped and de-limbed on site, the slash remained to provide nutrients and ground cover. The forest floor is surprisingly resilient, but the practice of clearcutting tends to increase the chance of erosion from heavy rains. The cause of the most severe erosion, however, is poor practices for building logging roads. The shortest distance between two points may have economic advantages for quickly removing timber, but it can be dev-

Sawyers cutting a log to length.
Courtesy of Library of Congress Photographs.

astating from an environmental standpoint. Roads were sometimes constructed straight up steep slopes, and those tracks were guaranteed to result in severe gullying. The goal of the company was to generate as much timber revenue as possible in the shortest amount of time. Long-term forest management was neither a common practice nor a high priority. In fact, the impact of those logging practices was not widely understood at that time.

In 1909 the Continental Company's operations manager, H.G. Frankenburger, created a detailed report for Schomburg listing the number of railroad ties alone that could be expected from each of the timber zones. The following excerpt shows some amazing totals, and

District	Number of Ties	Cost per Tie
Chase Canyon	80,000	27¢
Hainlein	30,000	26¢
Lower Cerrososo	25,000	27¢
McCrystal District	200,000	26¢
West of Rich Bros	70,000	27¢
Suree	60,000	27¢
Bonito	50,000	28¢
Dead Horse	60,000	28¢
Greenwood	35,000	30¢
Middle Ponil	175,000	30¢
Wilson Mesa	150,000	28¢
South Ponil	60,000	27¢
Dean Canyon	30,000	28¢
Cimarron to Ute Park	50,000	26¢
Cimarroncito	100,000	30¢
Upper Cerrososo	400,000	30¢
North Cerrososo Mesa	300,000	30¢
Van Bremmer District	150,000 to 200,000	34¢

it paints a picture of how dense the forest growth was at that time in each of these areas.

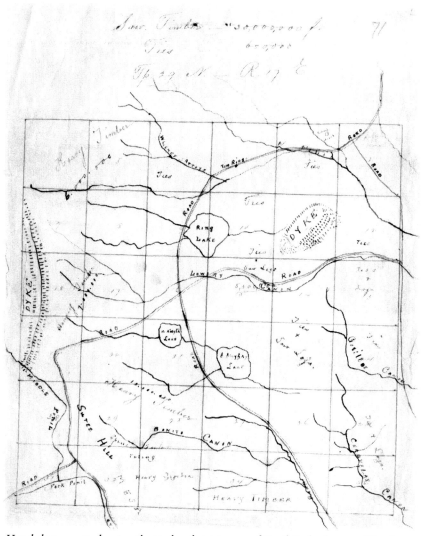

Hand-drawn map showing the timber districts west of Ponil Park, the type of lumber to be produced in each, and the locations of future roads and rail lines.
Courtesy of History Colorado Center: T.A. Schomburg Collection.

In many places throughout the Ponil canyons the company established small sawmills to pre-process lumber, especially for rough-cut boards. The ultimate destination for the timber was the central mill located at the end of the rail line in East Cimarron. There the company built an extensive track yard, drying facilities, planing mills, lumber treatment and packaging plants, warehouses, and offices.

Even before logging began in the Ponil country there were many families that lived in the region. According to the 1900 US census there were at least eighty people in the Ponil Park precinct before the C&N railroad even reached the area. With the coming of the railroad, however, Ponil Park quickly grew into a popular community at the railhead. In addition to the lumber yard there was a small depot, a US post office, a school, and a grocery store. Kermit Webster, who grew up in Ponil Park, commented that "it was a railroad stop and around in the hills there was lumber being made." He remembered that his mother had a small vegetable garden near their cabin, and that he enjoyed playing in the sawdust pile near the mill. "I had my first bottle of soda pop there. It was a gift from the man who owned the grocery store."

Loaded logging wagons with Ponil Park in the background.
Courtesy of Raton Museum.

Several miles west of Ponil Park in what was then known as Lowery Cañon (Sealy Canyon today), an extension of the C&N rails followed the creek to another large sawmill constructed by Pratt and Woods. A community with over thirty buildings grew at this location, and they named it Ring after the former owner of the property, Timothy Ring, whose log house was two miles to the north. In just a few short years the C&N line would be extended further to the south from this point in order to harvest the rich timber in the Bonita Canyon area.

Due to a slump in lumber prices the early years of the operation were not as profitable as expected, but even in 1907 before the C&N railroad had been completed the Continental Company was able to pay a $6,000 royalty to the Maxwell Company. The next year that royalty had increased to $16,000 and by 1910 they paid $87,943 in

Men and logs on Christmas Day at Ring, New Mexico.
Courtesy of Old Mill Museum.

royalties alone. During the following decade the Continental Tie and Lumber Company was consistently profitable, mainly because the supply of fine timber in the area seemed inexhaustible.

Thomas Schomburg's original prediction was accurate, however, and at the end of twenty years the usable timber was growing thin. The rail line had been extended into some remote areas, but transportation costs began to exceed returns. By 1923 the company had abandoned its line to Ponil Park and had removed the rails and equipment. They used this equipment to build along the south and middle forks of the Ponil until they reached the base of Wilson Mesa. By this time, however, the gasoline-powered truck had become available, and these new vehicles proved to be a more efficient way to remove the timber. The short haul railroad was becoming obsolete.

At the beginning of the Great Depression the demand for lumber completely disappeared. In 1930 the Continental Tie and Lumber Company dismantled the Cimarron & Northwestern railway, officially suspending the corporation on December 1, 1931. By this time the Maxwell Company had sold much of this property to private owners, and extensive logging operations were no longer possible. The days of logging on a massive scale had come to an end, and the forest was left to begin its growth cycle anew.

Waite Phillips and the Philmont Ranch

Waite Phillips first heard about the Cimarron country of northeastern New Mexico in the spring of 1922. Gene Hayward, the manager of the Highland Ranch that Phillips owned south of Denver, had been looking for several months for another ranch for Phillips, one which had more mountainous country for recreational opportunities for him and his family.

Hayward had been drawn to Cimarron because of the proposed sale of 42,000 acres of the Urraca Ranch. After inspecting the property, he sent a report to Phillips about the ranch's choice grazing and irrigated farming acres along the foothills and mountains of the Sangre de Cristo range. In addition, the ranch was well watered with several streams that flowed out of the mountains to the west.

Phillips was intrigued with Hayward's report and decided to make his own inspection. Afterward, he came away with an agreement to purchase the Urraca property for a little over $150,000. A year later he bought another 30,000 acres of the ranch for a quarter of a million dollars. The ranch provided an excellent foundation on which Phillips was able to expand his holdings. As contiguous property became available, he bought it. By the end of 1926 he had put almost 300,000 acres under one fence.

Aside from the scenic mountains and lush cattle range, Phillips was attracted to the Cimarron country by its colorful history. Cimarron had been the headquarters of mountain man Lucien Maxwell's ranch

From "Waite Phillips and the Philmont Ranch" by Stephen Zimmer, *Philmont: An Illustrated History*, Irving, Texas: Boy Scouts of America, 1988: 23-41.

Early photo of Garcia Cow Camp on La Grulla Mesa.
Courtesy of Philmont Scout Ranch.

on the old Beaubien and Miranda Land Grant in the 1860s, and it had been an important stop on the Santa Fe Trail. Maxwell's friend Kit Carson had been a frequent visitor. A gold rush occurred in the mountains on the western part of the ranch in 1866. After several years of investing in mining, Maxwell sold the ranch to speculators in 1870. The sale precipitated a bloody settlers' war, known as the Colfax County War, in which gunslinger Clay Allison played a dominant role. Waite Phillips enjoyed owning a piece of history.

Eventually Phillips stocked his ranch with more than 3,000 head of Hereford cows and 9,000 head of Corriedale sheep. At first he named the ranch Hawkeye Ranch, in honor of his native state of Iowa. But in 1925 he coined the name Philmont, which he derived by combining his name and the Spanish word for mountain. He applied to the New Mexico Livestock Board for a W P connected brand for his cows, but he was informed that the brand was already in use. Instead he chose and received a double U bar brand for cattle and the W P connected for horses.

During the previous ten years Phillips had operated a diversified oil company out of Tulsa, Oklahoma, and had only recently invested in ranch property with the purchase of the Highland Ranch a few years before. Since he did not have a great deal of experience in the cattle business, he carefully studied all aspects of modern livestock management. He brought to this work the same energy and managerial skill that led to his success in the oil business.

Immediately after buying the ranch, Phillips began developing its resources as they pertained to livestock, farming, and recreation. Although an absentee owner, Phillips kept in close touch with all activity on the ranch. Over the years of his ownership he required ranch managers to send him weekly reports about weather conditions and current operations in the cow, horse, sheep, and farming departments, plus information about personnel, water, and fencing. Phillips meticulously responded to the reports and offered suggestions for specific actions and possible solutions to problems.

Philmont Ranch cowboy Buck Ray in 1932.
Courtesy of Philmont Scout Ranch.

No aspect of the ranch's operation escaped his attention. He was especially concerned with the welfare of his employees. On average the ranch employed as many as fifty people, including ten cowboys, fifteen sheepherders, twenty farmers along with office and maintenance personnel. Each employee was supplied a house, milk cow, garden seed, poultry stock, beef, and pork. In a May 1936 letter to the ranch manager, Phillips stated that the ranch furnished "to its employees as nearly as possible what they would received if they owned or leased a small place of their own."

Perhaps the greatest contribution Phillips made to the ranch's cattle operation was his plan for managing the cow herd and utilizing the available range grass. The plan involved developing springs and other water sources and using cross-fences and strategic salt distributions to entice cattle to graze the less accessible parts of the ranch.

Philmont cows calved each spring from the middle of March to the middle of May while pastured on sheltered lowlands. During the first part of June the cowboys began gathering cows and

Cowboy Malaques Espinosa at Philmont Ranch.
Courtesy of Philmont Scout Ranch.

George Rockenfield oversees a mowing operation at Philmont Ranch.
Courtesy of Philmont Scout Ranch.

calves along with the herd bulls and pushed them in bunches of three hundred to Zastro, a trap at the foot of the mountains in the southern part of the ranch.

After overnighting them there, the cowboys drove the cattle up the steep, rocky trail to the summer mountain pastures of La Grulla, Agua Fria, and Garcia Parks, situated at elevations of over 9,000 feet. The older cows needed little encouragement to climb on top having been conditioned by the drive many times before.

At the head of the drive the cows were met by another crew of cowboys, who held them at La Grulla Park, paired them up, and branded the calves. Each bunch was held in the big open park, and the ropers necked the calves in order to drag them to the fire. Following branding, the cows and calves were pushed to the western edge of the pastures and then allowed to drift back eastward to lower elevations as summer progressed.

All cows, calves, and bulls were gathered from the high country by the end of September. After the calves were weaned in October, they were driven to Cimarron and loaded on a branch line of the Santa Fe Railroad for the long ride to market in Kansas City.

In the early years of the ranch the remuda was supplied with outside purchases of broke cow horses. But in the late 1920s Phillips bought a dozen thoroughbred race mares off the track at Tiajuana, Mexico, for the foundation of a horse breeding program. Eventually the broodmare band grew to more than a hundred head, not all of which were full thoroughbreds.

These mares were matched with a number of stallions including the Quarter Horse foundation sire, Plaudit, acquired in 1933, and thor-

Philmont Ranch manager Roy Lewis mounted on Plaudit.
Courtesy of Philmont Scout Ranch.

oughbred stallions Lani Chief, Prince James, Stall Star, and Stevenson II. All of them produced some colts that either went to the track or the polo field, whereas most of their get proved their worth as cow horses in the rough mountains of the ranch. Each spring all of the three-year-old colts were started by the horse department, and those destined for the cow outfit were sent to the cowboys in time for the spring and late summer riding.

Phillips' son Elliott spent summers as a teenager at the ranch with the cow outfit. Although he was the owner's son, he made a regular hand and relished the time horseback and staying in the mountain camps. Several years ago he described life on the ranch with the cowboy crew:

> We went everywhere horseback. Each man had at least six horses in his string. It took that many to stand the twenty-five to thirty-five miles we rode each day. We changed horses sometime during the day if we could, but most of the time we were working too far from camp to get back and eat, let alone change horses.
>
> We worked seven days a week from daylight until the work was finished. Sometimes we were through by three or four o'clock, but often it was after dark when we finally rode into camp. We seldom ate

Philmont Ranch cattle being loaded into AT&SF cattle cars at Cimarron.
Courtesy of Philmont Scout Ranch.

more than twice a day, but no one complained. There was something about cowboying.

Each man took pride in his work and his ability to withstand considerable punishment, whether riding a bucking horse or staying out all day in the rain. To be a part of that was a wonderful experience. I guess it spoiled me for any other line of work. I've tried other occupations, but my main interest has been ranching, and I've been at it for more than sixty years.

After owning the Philmont for twenty years, in 1941 Waite Phillips gave the mountainous part of the ranch to the Boy Scouts of America, known today as Philmont Scout Ranch, for a wilderness camping area. His only stipulations were that he and his family be able to ride on the ranch whenever they visited and that his favorite horse, Gus, be turned out and allowed to live out his life without being ridden.

Philmont Ranch cowboy crew in 1933.
Courtesy of Philmont Scout Ranch.

Cow Ranch to Polo Field

Polo is the fastest team sport in the world. It holds preeminence in speed because the legs of the player are those of the horse he rides. After its introduction to the United States in 1876, polo had gained well-deserved recognition as a national sport by 1920. Over the next two decades spectators by the thousands thronged to Eastern polo fields to watch the daring, wide-open play of high goal sportsmen mounted on horses of uncanny athletic ability and speed.

As the game developed in the United States, players increasingly refined the techniques of both individual and team play. Moreover, they brought to the game better bred and faster horses that dramatically increased the pace. Players demanded the fastest horses capable of playing the game—a fast horse meant reaching the ball before an opponent, or at the very least, maneuvering quickly to catch him out of position.

From the earliest years various cattle ranches throughout the West supplied a large number of horses for the game. A western cow horse was a natural, possessed of the intelligence, athletic ability, and courage necessary to play the game. Nevertheless, western cow horses were generally small, having descended from range mustangs and, consequently, were comparatively slow.

The thoroughbred racing horse did meet the players' requirements for speed. With the growing popularity of the sport and the demand for faster horses, many western cattlemen began bringing thorough-

From "Breeding Fleet Polo Steeds" by Stephen Zimmer, *Polo Magazine*,
Vol. 22, No. 4, September 1996: 18-20.

bred blood onto their ranches for the purpose of breeding up their brood bands and selling the outstanding offspring for the game of polo. In the process, ranches found that any horses unable to make the grade for polo and other equestrian sports often made the best mounts for their cowboys to use in cattle work.

In 1930 Will Rogers, an enthusiastic proponent and player of polo, commented in his newspaper column that many of the polo ponies used by teams in the East had been bred and trained on western ranches. He felt that the game of polo had "done more to establish the breeding of good horses" in the West than even horse racing had.

Horse breeders in West Texas were at the vanguard of raising and training ponies for use by clubs in the East. In New Mexico, two large ranches situated at the foot of the Sangre de Cristo mountains near Cimarron followed suit by up-breeding their horse herds with the intent of marketing both young horses and seasoned mounts for polo, jumping, and the US Cavalry.

The CS Cattle Company, managed by Edward Springer, along with the neighboring Philmont Ranch, owned by Oklahoma oilman Waite

Early Philmont Ranch advertisement for polo ponies.

Phillips, began raising thoroughbred and part-thoroughbred horses in the 1920s. When cattle prices plummeted at the outset of the Great Depression, these cattlemen accelerated their horse breeding programs and used them as sources of important income.

The economic incentives were substantial. Whereas a good cow horse might sell for $100 to $150 at the beginning of the Depression, a polo prospect—a young horse untrained for the game but having the proper conformation and breeding—might go for as much as $300, while a seasoned, well-trained mount would bring much more.

Both the CS and Philmont ranches made concerted efforts to

1935 Polo Team, Philmont Ranch.

promote their horses by advertising in various sports and horse-related publications. They also produced local polo shows and tournaments where the buying public could see firsthand the training and breeding of their horses. By the beginning of the Depression, the Springer thoroughbred and better-bred mares numbered over 200 head and were producing colts that displayed the conformation, disposition, and speed to make them capable of playing international polo, working cows, or serving in the cavalry.

The US Army's Western Remount Service aided the CS and Philmont breeding programs by allotting them seventeen thoroughbred stallions during the 1930s. In exchange for the services of these studs, each ranch agreed to sell certain horses from the resulting get to the Army for cavalry mounts. With its potential for bringing in additional revenue and for upgrading breeding herds, this program was popular on ranches throughout the West. Many of the horses selected were taken by officers as polo mounts and used by Army teams at posts scattered across the country.

Success in selling horses for whatever purpose depended not only on their breeding, but on skillfully handling them during the crucial period while they were still colts. Colts that demonstrated the disposition and conformation to make polo mounts were put to saddle as three-year-olds. After they responded to bridle and bit and had learned to handle their feet under the weight of a rider, they underwent preliminary training on the polo field to accustom them to the ball and mallet. In their fourth year they were ridden in slow practice games where they learned to play the game under the tutelage of a patient

Cimarron Polo Pony Show
June 30th, 1935
EVENTS FOR POLO PONIES, POLO
PROSPECTS, REMOUNTS, HUNTERS,
AND COW PONIES

POLO TOURNAMENT
July 1st, 2nd, and 3rd
SEVERAL VISITING TEAMS COMPETING

Cimarron Rodeo
July 4th
No Charge for General Admission
BIGGER AND BETTER THAN EVER
EIGHT HORSE RACES, BRONC RIDING,
ROPING, WILD COW MILKING AND
FULL QUOTA OF COWBOY EVENTS
Sponsored by
MAVERICK CLUB OF CIMARRON
EVERYBODY WELCOME

1935 advertisement for the Cimarron Rodeo, featuring polo ponies.

rider. In the meantime, they were often given to the ranch cowboys to develop as cow horses.

Some horses were sold in the fall of their first year of training. The more precocious, however, were held back for several seasons of subsequent play at which time they were sold for higher prices as seasoned polo mounts. Beginning in 1934 the CS and Philmont ranches inaugurated a series of horse shows in Cimarron to promote the sale of their horses. The first, held on June 17, 1934, drew 4,000 breeders, buyers, and spectators from all over the country. A full range of competitive events for polo, polo-prospect, and cavalry mounts were featured. A local men's group, the Cimarron Maverick Club, helped sponsor the event along with the United States Polo Association which donated $200 as the show's prize money. In addition to show events, a polo tournament was staged following the opening day performance, for the purpose of demonstrating the abilities of the horses rather than the talents of individual players or teams.

As a result of the success of the first Cimarron Polo Show, Waite Phillips donated a tract of land in Cimarron to the Maverick Club for a polo field, arena, and rodeo grounds. For his part, Ed Springer built nearby barns, club rooms, and other facilities. In the spring of 1935 the arena was prepared for another show in June.

Participation in the 1935 Cimarron Horse Show exceeded that of the previous year. The *Raton Range* reported that the 1935 show demonstrated again to "dealers and players East, West, and Far West that the ponies [in the Cimarron district] were capable of playing in the fastest company."

Late that summer Ed Springer of the CS Ranch, Roy Lewis, Philmont Ranch manager, and Brownlow Wilson of the WS Ranch and general manager of the 1935 show, established the Cimarron Polo Club.

The club served as an official body to promote the sale of locally raised and trained polo ponies through sponsorship of polo games and horse shows.

To demonstrate the breeding and training of their polo ponies to a wider audience, the CS Ranch entered the Colorado Springs Broadmoor Hotel polo tournament in August 1936. The CS players won the finals of the Lyle Cup on August 11th at Penrose Park Field against a team sponsored by the Broadmoor Hotel. The Colorado Springs *Gazette* reported that the CS team rode "exceptionally fast mounts and as a result...outrode and outplayed the Broadmoor quartet." The next weekend the CS team again defeated the Broadmoor in the finals of the Penrose Polo Cup by a score of 10-8. The Broadmoor tournament marked the end of the polo season along the front range of the Rockies, and the play of the horses and riders from the CS drew further national attention to Cimarron's polo activities.

Cimarron Polo Club on their playing field about 1935.

In the summer of 1937 a unique ranch was established south of Cimarron based on the village's reputation as a polo breeding and training center. Founded as the Vallejo Polo Ranch, its operation initially centered on schooling polo prospects for the game, but after a year of operation, it expanded to include a players' school where aspiring poloists could learn the fundamentals and horsemanship of the game.

The ranch founder, an English sportsman and poloist named W.L. Horbury, created a guest ranch atmosphere for the players, providing them with comfortable lodgings and varied leisure-time activities. Vallejo advertised with the slogan, "We train both man and horse," and urged potential students to combine instruction in polo form and fun-

The famous CS Ranch pony, Breeches, who competed on several eastern polo teams.

damentals with a pleasant summer vacation.

By the end of the 1930s it seemed that the Cimarron district was destined to rival West Texas as the major polo pony breeding and training area in the United States. The CS and Philmont ranches continued producing horse shows and selling polo ponies in the pre-war years, but as fighting increased in Europe, more and more of their potential polo mounts were diverted for sale to the horse cavalry of the US Army as it prepared for possible deployment. American involvement in World War II dealt a crippling blow to polo nationwide as both players and horses were called up for military service and most clubs were disbanded.

After the bombing of Pearl Harbor, the CS turned its full attention away from horses toward cattle production to support the war effort. At the same time, the status of the Philmont Ranch changed. In late 1941 Waite Phillips deeded a major portion of the ranch to the Boy Scouts of America as a national wilderness camp that became Philmont Scout Ranch. The rest of the ranch was sold to an Arizona cattleman, while the majority of the Philmont mares were sold to outside breeders.

American polo has in recent year regained much of its popularity, and although the Cimarron ranches are no longer a part, many of the game's horses continue to be raised and trained in the West. Although scattered throughout the country, the CS and Philmont mares and stallions left an important legacy in the modern horse world. This legacy displays the same intelligence, athletic ability, and conformation of their forebears, and they have in their own right exhibited top performance not only on ranches but in national racing, cutting, and horse show events as well.

Vermejo Park Ranch

In 1887 the Maxwell Land Grant Company estimated that more than 65,000 head of cattle and 15,000 head of sheep were pastured on company lands, mostly along the Vermejo River. After negotiating agreements with all of the ranchers, the company was able to offer large sections of its range land for sale.

One of the first buyers was Harold Wilson, an Englishman who had been ranching in southwestern New Mexico Territory with his partner, Montague Stevens. The two men had been searching for range they could fence in order to better protect their WS-branded cattle. In 1899 they bought 125,000 acres situated between the Ponil and Vermejo Rivers and added an additional 30,000 acres a year later. The Maxwell lands that became the WS Ranch comprised a rectangle thirty miles long by ten miles wide. It was fenced with more than one hundred miles of barbed wire and was the first ranch on the grant to be so enclosed.

As a result of promotional efforts, demand for Maxwell range land increased. William Bartlett, a grain dealer from Chicago, responded to one of the company's ads in the fall of 1900, inquiring about ranch acreage as well as land suitable for hunting and fishing. After inspecting the Maxwell land in 1901, Bartlett bought 220,000 acres centered in what was known as Vermejo Park. The mountainous areas were priced at thirty cents an acre, while the parks and pastures sold for a little

Adapted from "Vermejo Park: A History of a New Mexico Ranch"
by Stephen Zimmer, *Ranch Record*, January 2009: 14-16.

The cattle operation at Vermejo Park Ranch in the early 1900s.

more than a dollar per acre. The following year Bartlett began to build a mountain retreat by constructing a cottage for his family on the north side of the Vermejo River. Afterward, Bartlett's sons, Norman and William, Jr., lived on the ranch while their father directed activities from Chicago.

Bartlett's partner in the cattle operation was H.W. Adams who built the ranch's herds primarily with cattle purchased from stockmen who had dropped their leases on the Maxwell Land Grant. Within five years the Adams Company cattle, carrying an A6 brand, numbered more than 6,000 head.

Adams established his headquarters on the south side of the Vermejo River upstream from Bartlett's cottage and built houses for himself and his range foreman, along with a bunkhouse for the cowboys. In addition he constructed barns and corrals, and he began cultivating fields along the river to raise hay.

Interior view of living area at Casa Grande.

In 1907 Bartlett expanded his original cottage in a grandiose manner. The finished structure was a massive, twenty bedroom stone edifice that he called Casa Grande. Bartlett's oldest son, Norman, and his wife lived on the second floor, while another house named Casa Minor was built next door for his younger son, William, Jr. Eventually construction also began on a residence for Bartlett himself. When it was completed in 1910, Bartlett retired from his Chicago business and moved to the ranch permanently, bringing along a 12,000-volume library.

Bartlett loved to ride, hunt, and fish on the ranch, as well as to entertain his friends and business associates in the backcountry. In 1912 he described himself as being "a cattleman in

William Bartlett seated in his favorite rocking chair by the fireplace at his Castle Rock Park lodge.

the mountains of New Mexico with a ranch half the size of the State of Rhode Island and cattle on a thousand hills…I have ten or twelve thousand books here with me along with horses to ride, streams and lakes to fish, and the most glorious climate under heaven. The scenery of the old world cannot equal Vermejo."

Unfortunately, Bartlett's fairy tale life as a gentleman rancher ended when he died abruptly in December 1918. He left the ranch to his eldest son, Norman, who unexpectedly passed away only a year later. Norman, in turn, left the property to his brother William, who only enjoyed it for a year until he also died. William's wife, Virginia, kept the ranch until 1926 when she deeded it to The Vermejo Club, a corporation organized as an exclusive hunting, fishing, and recreation association.

William Bartlett's immense Casa Grande mansion at Vermejo Park.

Lavish Vermejo Club living room inside Casa Grande.

Harry Chandler, owner of the *Los Angeles Times* newspaper, was the driving force behind the Vermejo Club. In addition to being a newspaper publisher Chandler was building one of the largest real estate empires in the nation, being widely known for developing Hollywood and the San Fernando valley of southern California. Membership in the Vermejo Club was by invitation only, and the fee was $1,000 a year. Many prominent people joined, including President Herbert Hoover, industrialists Harvey Firestone and Andrew Mellon, film moguls Cecil B. deMille and Thomas W. Warner, and movie stars Douglas Fairbanks and Mary Pickford.

The mansions built by Bartlett served as guest houses and lodges. A landing strip was constructed so members could fly into the remote property, and they could choose to stay in an isolated cottage or to enjoy the tennis courts and pool tables in the luxurious headquarters facilities. The club disbanded during the depression of the 1930s because its members were not able to maintain their contributions. Harry Chandler attempted to sustain the club by having one of his companies take ownership of the land. The Southwest Land Company closed the mansions, but it leased the grazing land to Ira Aten for several years as a cattle range.

It appeared that the days of the Vermejo Park Ranch resort were over, but in 1945 W.J. Gourley, an industrialist from Ft. Worth, became interested in ranch country in northeastern New Mexico. He first bought the old WS Ranch and then added Bartlett's Vermejo Park property three years later. Gourley continued acquiring adjoining ranch land until he had more than 480,000 acres under one fence. He stocked the combined ranches with cattle and branded them with the historic WS brand.

The Gourleys enjoyed the ranch until he passed away in August 1970. Subsequently, his wife was unsuccessful in her attempts to sell the ranch either to the state of New Mexico or to the United States government. In 1973 she finally reached an agreement with the Pennzoil Corporation of Houston to take over the ranch.

During Pennzoil's ownership, hunting and fishing continued on the ranch along with the cattle operation. In January 1982 Pennzoil donated 100,000 acres of the ranch to the United States Forest Service, which represented the largest private land gift ever made to the USFS. To offset the donation, in 1989 Pennzoil bought 190,000 acres adjoining the north part of the ranch and added it to Vermejo, bringing the ranch's total acreage to more than 600,000 acres.

In 1996 Vermejo Park once again changed hands when Ted Turner of Atlanta added it to the list of ranches he already owned in the West. Soon afterward, Turner directed the ranch's cowboys to gather the cattle off the range and bring in 1,200 bison to take their place. Most of these impressive creatures were turned out onto the historic WS range northeast of Cimarron where their ancestors had grazed two hundred years before. Today, Vermejo Park pastures the largest privately owned bison herd in the United States.

Vermejo Park cowboys still ride the ranch on horses. Although they no longer brand in the spring, they have conditioned the bison horseback in order to gather them for the spring and fall work. It is a gentle and fitting way to handle them that has proven to be less stressful than using the modern four wheeler. To this day, the Vermejo Park area is one of the most beautiful spots in the vast Cimarron country.

Photo of elk grazing in Vermejo Park, early 1900s.

Water for a Dry and Thirsty Land

The Cimarron country has always been known as a land in need of water. August has the highest average moisture total, but even that equates to less than three and a half inches of rain for the entire month. Everything that lives in this land has adapted to the dry conditions, and many plants and animals thrive there. In fact, part of the beauty and appeal of the Cimarron country can be directly traced to the unique climate of this area.

Like much of the land along the eastern foothills of the Rocky Mountains, this region was labeled as "desert." When the territory to the north first became part of the United States after the Louisiana Purchase in 1803, President Thomas Jefferson described it as covered with "immense and trackless deserts." In the journal of his 1806 expedition, Lieutenant Zebulon Pike wrote, "These vast plains of the western hemisphere may become in time equally celebrated as the sandy deserts of Africa." His 1807 map of the Spanish territory that he passed through included a note in the area around the Cimarron country which reads, "Immense dry plains."

In 1820 Major Stephen Long led the first scientific expedition to the headwaters of the South Platte River and into the central Rockies. He reached the headwaters of the Arkansas and descended that river on his return to the States. Writing of the high prairies east of the mountains, expedition scientist Edwin James concluded, "I do not hesitate in giving the opinion that it is almost wholly unfit for cultivation, and

By Steve Lewis

Stephen H. Long's 1820 map showing the Cimarron Country as part of the "Great Desert."

Courtesy of Library of Congress Geography and Map Division.

of course uninhabitable by a people depending upon agriculture for their subsistence. Although tracts of fertile land are occasionally to be met with, yet the scarcity of wood and water will prove an insuperable obstacle to settling the country." Major Long's highly publicized map from the expedition shows the label "Great Desert" printed along the area east of the mountains, which includes the Cimarron country.

The early official reports were unanimous in concluding that the high prairies were not suited for agriculture. This might have been because all these assessments were made by people only familiar with farming east of the 100th meridian. Conditions in the West were quite unlike anything they considered normal. What they failed to realize was that farming had been practiced in New Mexico for generations, using techniques originally employed by the ancient native peoples.

When Spaniards first entered the Rio Grande valley in the early 1600s, they found many villages surrounded by cultivated fields. The natives used *acequias* or irrigation canals to distribute ground water from rivers and streams. This allowed them not only to raise grain and grow fruit, but even to cultivate flower gardens.

As new settlers from the east began moving west, they brought their eastern farming methods with them. Unfortunately, they soon discovered that traditional techniques would not make the land productive. Only when they studied the methods of their native neighbors did they

Rainfall totals west of the 100th meridian required very different farming techniques.

begin to raise crops successfully. The soil was rich, but irrigation was required to compensate for the lack of natural rainfall. Ground water had to be carefully conserved and managed, putting every last drop to productive use.

All of the early gardens and farms in the Cimarron country used water from the creeks and streams. Sometimes water was carried to a garden using bags or buckets, while larger cultivated plots were often watered by digging narrow ditches to divert the flow of a creek. By the mid-1800s, successful farms had been established on the Vermejo, Ponil, Cimarron, Cimarroncito, Urraca, and Rayado streams.

The first large influx of settlers came west to take up homesteads east of the Colorado foothills in the early 1860s, initially attracted by the gold rush in the mountains west of Denver. Through trial and error they began using irrigation ditches to make their land productive, and these original property owners wanted the protection of the law for their investments and construction projects. Eastern water law, termed Riparian Rights, allocated water only to those who owned the land bordering the water source. In the semi-arid West, however, water was often moved great distances from its source. It soon became apparent that new laws were needed to regulate and protect western water rights.

The people of Colorado Territory tackled this issue in the early 1870s. Colorado Supreme Court Chief Justice Moses Hallett wrote in 1872, "In a dry and thirsty land it is necessary to divert the waters of the streams from the natural channels, in order to obtain the fruits of the soil, and this necessity is so universal that it claims recognition of the law." The Colorado system, which became known as the doctrine of Prior Appropriation, worked well and was applied in all of the neighboring western states including New Mexico.

Essentially, Prior Appropriation uncoupled water rights from property ownership. The first person to use water from the source for a "beneficial purpose" was given the right to continue using that amount of water for that purpose. Later users were allowed to request rights to the remaining water for their own beneficial purposes, as long as they did not take water that had been granted to previous holders.

Irrigation water was used to "reclaim" arid land for farming, and eventually the government would establish a Bureau of Reclamation to fund larger projects for managing and conserving scarce western water. In the Cimarron country, however, reclamation efforts were left in private hands. During the 1880s many large "colonization" schemes had been attempted in several western states, and one essential element for their success was a colony or company sponsored canal and ditch system. After the Maxwell Land Grant Company became the major property holder in the Cimarron country, its managers followed the example of these previous colony efforts in order to attract settlers.

With the arrival of the railroad, the Maxwell company began promoting its prairie acreage as farm land. This happened to coincide with a relatively wet decade in terms of rainfall. Some pundits even concluded that the "rain belt" was moving west. One railroad promotional brochure made these exaggerated claims in 1882:

> In our opinion, the change is due to the extensive irrigation of land lying along the eastern base of the Rocky Mountains. Great rivers, which head in perpetual snow banks, have been turned into irrigation ditches, and the water which formerly ran wastefully into the Gulf of Mexico has been turned onto the arid plains. There it soaks into the soil. The wind sweeping over the land sucks up a large portion of it. There is then moisture in the air and it is precipitated on the high prairies.

Irrigation projects became very popular throughout the West, and in 1887 the Maxwell Company employed an experienced water engineer, E.H. Kellogg, to survey the area. Based on his favorable report, land speculators began leasing large sections of the prairie. M.W. Mills contracted for 100,000 acres near the AT&SF rail line, hoping to convince settlers to pay $15 an acre for the property. Mills eventually gained the support of a group of Chicago businessmen who invested $60,000 to construct a ditch system for water diverted from the Cimarron River. They organized the Springer Land Association, but their financial and promotional difficulties resulted in the property being returned to the

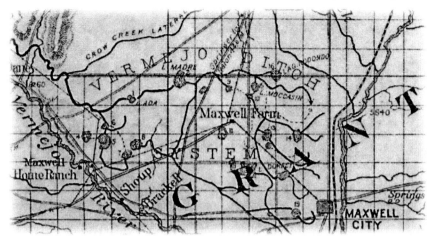

Maxwell Land Grant map of the Vermejo Ditch System west of Maxwell City, showing canals, laterals, and twenty reservoirs for retaining water.
Courtesy of Old Mill Museum.

Maxwell Company in 1891.

Meanwhile, engineer E.H. Kellogg had convinced the Maxwell managers that a similar ditch system on the Vermejo River could irrigate thousands of additional acres of farmland. They approved the project in July 1888, predicting that land under this system would sell for $25 per acre. Several groups of German and Russian immigrants visited the property in 1889, but many were discouraged because farm land was not located near an established town. To remedy this situation, the company organized the Maxwell City Land and Improvement Company to build a new town near the ditch system. By the end of 1890 Maxwell City had a railroad depot and a large stone mercantile building. However, acreage that did sell brought only $5 or $6 per acre.

In 1891 a group of Colorado speculators, represented by Stephen W. Dorsey, expressed an interest in building a dam and irrigation ditches in the Moreno Valley south of Elizabethtown. They believed such a system could irrigate at least 40,000 acres, and they offered to purchase the Springer ditches as part of the deal. Unfortunately, the plan fell through when Dorsey failed to raise the needed capital in the days leading up to the nationwide financial panic of 1893.

Around this time the wet weather cycle also came to an end, and the worst drought this area had ever seen occurred in 1894. Even though land sales were at an all-time low, there were already 1,000 cultivated acres under the Springer ditch system and 4,000 under the Vermejo system. The Maxwell company had agreed to maintain the ditches, and their maintenance costs rose to several thousand dollars each year. In addition to these expenses, the company had grossly over-estimated the number of acres that could be irrigated by both systems. There was only one year, for example, when the Vermejo system supplied enough water to irrigate 5,000 acres. In their search for ways to make the land profitable, the company experimented with sugar beets in 1900. By the following summer they were sending a crop of beets to market, but during the drought of 1902 the Vermejo River could barely supply enough water to irrigate 2,000 acres.

Farmers were upset by the water shortages and the Maxwell Company wanted to rid itself of properties requiring expensive maintenance, so in 1904 the operation of the system was turned over to the local community. Through a series of financial transactions during the next several years, all of the water rights and ditch systems were assigned to the newly organized Maxwell Irrigated Land Company.

The official 1909 report of the New Mexico Territorial Engineer listed about 22,000 acres west of Maxwell City owned by the Maxwell Irrigated Land Company, in addition to forty or fifty miles of ditches and laterals. This company also acquired all the stock of the Vermejo Ditch Company, which held the oldest water rights on the Vermejo River.

The community began to see results, and by 1910 they were shipping sugar beets at the rate of several freight cars per week. Land values remained steady, and the community grew and prospered through 1914. Later that year, however, the dam failed on one of the system's major reservoirs. This effectively crippled the Vermejo ditch system, resulting in almost constant water shortages afterward. By 1916 many families left and the community slowly withered.

Produce displayed by the Maxwell Irrigated Land Company.

During the years preceding New Mexico statehood, the population of the territory continued to grow. This prompted the territorial legislature to draft a much-needed irrigation law. Their 1907 statute established the office of Territorial Engineer, which would conduct water surveys and determine fair allocation of water rights. In order to obtain new water rights a person could apply for a permit from the Territorial Engineer, who determined whether any unappropriated water was available and if the applicant would put the water to beneficial use.

Irrigation canal on the Vermejo Ditch System near the Maxwell Experimental Station.

Some of the most successful water storage projects in the Cimarron country were those developed by Charles Springer, owner of the CS Ranch. His reservoirs on the Ponil and Vermejo streams were located in the mountains, rather than on the plains. These man-made lakes were at higher altitudes and were deeper than typical irrigation ponds, so there was less water lost to evaporation. This also allowed the high mesas to be irrigated, where eventually the water would return to creeks and could be reused for irrigating prairie farms downstream. The New Mexico Territorial Engineer commented on this method, saying that "the greatest duty of water can be obtained by using it on lands nearest the source, thereby not only economizing it best in the first use, but also permitting the use of the return water several times over."

Encouraged by his successes, Charles Springer resurrected the earlier idea for building a dam at the head of Cimarron Canyon in order to form a lake in Moreno Valley. A deep reservoir of that size at that altitude would potentially meet the needs of a very large population. Springer and other investors formed the Cimarron Valley Land Company in 1907, and they were granted New Mexico water permit #71 for their project. Vernon L. Sullivan, the Territorial Engineer in 1909, wrote to the US Secretary of Agriculture:

> The Cimarron project, known also as the Eagles Nest project, has probably the best reservoir site in New Mexico. The Cimarron River, after passing through the mountains, enters a narrow valley with high mountains on every side. At this place a dam is to be constructed 130 feet high, impounding 113,700 acre-feet for the irrigation of 65,000 acres. The estimated cost of the work is $100,000.

It took almost a decade of financial dealing and litigation before construction could begin on the dam, but by 1920 the project was

Eagle Nest dam, showing that the reservoir had filled to capacity by 1922.
Courtesy of Philmont Scout Ranch.

completed at a cost well over the estimate. The resulting lake in Moreno Valley is five miles long, two miles wide, and now holds about 70,000 acre feet of water. Water rights were sold to several area ranchers, organizations, and municipalities. Some of the largest rights holders include the CS Cattle Company and several other ranching families, the cities of Raton, Springer, Eagle Nest, and Angel Fire, and recipients of deeds through Waite Phillips, including Philmont Scout Ranch, UU Bar Ranch, and Vermejo Park Ranch.

At the time of its completion, Charles Springer considered the project a financial failure. But through the years the water from this reservoir has served the needs of tens of thousands of residents in northeastern New Mexico. In 2002 the State of New Mexico purchased the reservoir, and in 2006 a landmark water rights settlement was mediated by the governor of New Mexico. Charles Springer's grand enterprise, located on the western edge of the Cimarron country, is still the largest privately built dam in the United States, providing water for a dry and thirsty land.

Coal Mining and Dawson

Coal was recognized as an abundant natural resource from the earliest days of settlement in the Cimarron country. During the 1860s both government and commercial survey crews reported that coal existed and was being used around the region. For example, the Kansas Pacific Railroad expedition of 1867 recorded,

> In the Raton Mountains [we] saw as many as twenty exposures of coal in at least a dozen different veins, the best of which was found in the cañons of the Vermejo and its branches, where were two beds of ten feet thickness, each admirably situated for cheap mining, and of great purity in respect of slate and sulphur. This coal, which is bituminous, is hauled in wagons 70 miles for the use of the government for blacksmithing purposes at Fort Union.

Cattleman John B. Dawson had passed through this region for several years when he delivered Texas cattle to the towns and gold camps of Colorado. He decided to establish his own ranch and to settle in the beautiful Vermejo Canyon area. At that time Lucien B. Maxwell was the sole owner of the vast Maxwell Land Grant, and Dawson purchased 3,700 acres of the Vermejo tract directly from Maxwell in 1869 for about a dollar an acre. He and his partners were successful at raising cattle and horses on this property for many years, and as a sideline they also continued to provide coal for their neighbors as the need arose.

In 1901 Dawson sold the coal-rich section of his ranch to the Dawson Fuel Company for a reported $400,000. This company had been

By Steve Lewis

*Interior of a
Dawson coal mine
(Stag Canyon Mine No. 4)*
Courtesy of Dawson
Association.

incorporated with funding from railroad interests in southern New Mexico and Texas, so a rail line was built from Tucumcari to Dawson for hauling the coal products to market. They immediately began developing the property by setting up a sawmill to produce lumber for buildings and the construction of mine workings. They built coke ovens in which coal is baked to form a concentrate which can be burned at much higher temperatures with very little smoke. By the end of 1901, the Dawson location had become a thriving coal camp with a population of several hundred people.

During the next few years Dawson grew into a full-fledged town, with an official US Post Office that would operate continuously for five decades. Frame cottages were built for the miners and their families, while the mines and processing facilities were also expanded to meet the rising demand. Coal mining has always been a dangerous business, and three men were killed late in 1903 when a fire broke out in one of the tunnels. Miraculously, 500 miners escaped unharmed, but fire crews worked for over a week to contain the blaze.

By 1905 the town had a hotel, school, general store, and a newspaper which served the needs of around 2,000 people. Even in those early days the residents claimed that Dawson was not a coal camp, but a real town—and if you said otherwise they would quickly set you straight. The success of the Dawson Fuel Company attracted the attention of the Phelps Dodge Corporation, one of the nation's largest mining companies, and in 1906 their subsidiary, the Stag Canyon Fuel Company, purchased all of the Dawson holdings.

In those days it was common practice for corporate mine owners to build company towns that would meet the needs of their employees. Mines were often located in remote areas with few existing facilities, and company towns seemed like the most efficient and convenient way to take care of workers and their families. They could live in nearby company housing, buy necessities at the local company store, and even be paid using 'scrip'—a company's own paper currency that could be redeemed at the company store. What may have been a convenience, however, was often viewed as a means of company control over workers by limiting their freedom.

Phelps Dodge was keenly aware of these issues, but it was determined to create a model town in which the company would exercise benevolent control over community life. Their overall philosophy was described in the official New Mexico publication for the 1915 Panama-California Exhibition:

> The new owners opened more mines, improved the equipment, installed more efficient apparatus, and particularly improved the status of the workers and created an *espirit de corps*, installing many splendid improvements in many ways. Good workmen draw good pay there, no one is overcharged at the company's store, and every possible effort is made to improve the men and their families, socially, mentally, and morally. More than all that, the waste of human life looked upon with such complacency in so many industrial quarters is something viewed with horror at Dawson. Safety is really first there. Nor is there any smack of paternalism in this. Good men, trained men, are worth money. The company finds it economical to keep the good ones on hand rather than train new ones. Hence the schools, the hospital, the theater, the good houses, and all the rest of it.

The company immediately proved to be as good as its word. One of the first buildings to be constructed in 1906 was a new hospital with two wards and seven private rooms, for a total of twenty-six beds. It contained offices, a surgery, X-ray room, laboratory, kitchen, and dining room—all of which were outfitted with the most modern equipment. Five doctors, two dentists, a registered pharmacist, and numerous nurses worked shifts in order to be available as needed. Medical care was provided free of charge to company employees and their families. Doctors

Dawson Hospital.
Courtesy of Dawson Association.

would also make house calls, and the physicians had a good reputation and rapport with the town residents. The medical staff also gave regular first aid classes, and it was said that "to wear a *Dawson First Aid* button is considered a distinction in any coal camp of the country."

A row of miners' cottages.
Courtesy of Raton Museum.

Several housing areas were constructed, each containing white frame cottages which the company rented to its employees. These neighborhoods were named after the mines, such as "Number Four," or after their location in the valley, such as Capitan Hill, Lauretta, or Railroad. Some of the houses were small, and because of housing shortages there were times when two families would share a four-room home. The typical rent for a company house in the 1920s was $8.50 per month, with all maintenance supplied free of charge by the company. Electricity was generated by a steam-powered electric plant, and each family was assessed $1.50 per month for this luxury.

Homes were heated using coal, coke, or wood—so coal bins were built behind each cottage. Outhouses were common, and it was not until the 1930s that homes came equipped with bathrooms and toilets. Over the years many families needed to switch houses as the number of children increased, and there was often a long waiting list of employees who wanted to move into larger quarters. Higher ranking workers or company managers were usually given the best homes.

The town's drinking water came from wells along the Vermejo River which were located upstream from Dawson, and the water was carried by gravity to a cistern at the top of the hill overlooking the town. Each household was assessed one dollar per month for water, no matter how much they used, and many families took advantage of this by planting large irrigated gardens in which they would grow vegetables for the family table. Doing laundry was a daily chore since a miner's clothes would accumulate irritating debris, and wash tubs with scrub boards were typically used to clean the clothes—although some homemakers had to boil the clothes in lye to get them clean.

Phelps Dodge Department Store. Courtesy of Dawson Association.

The original company store had been built in 1902, but in 1914 it was converted into a gym and recreation center. The new three-story Phelps Dodge Department Store replaced the old building, and this amazing edifice was at one time the largest department store in the state of New Mexico. It had large picture windows where merchandise was displayed, and the store's decorator received several national awards in recognition for this work. The main floor hosted departments for clothing and shoes, household goods, a pharmacy, grocery, and butcher shop. The mezzanine displayed furniture, while the bakery and managers' offices were on the top floor.

In the basement of this building there was an ice manufacturing plant where 5,000 pounds of ice were produced each day. Most families in Dawson had ice boxes in their homes rather than refrigerators, and the mercantile provided the ice required to keep their perishables fresh. A spur of the rail line ran behind the mercantile, and groceries were unloaded from refrigerated freight cars, rolled down ramps to the basement, where they were stored in giant coolers. The building had a hydraulic freight elevator powered by a series of valves and pumps which regulated water pressure to raise and lower the platform.

Education was very important to the citizens of Dawson, many of whom were recent immigrants to the United States. By 1915 there were four school buildings, including the Central School near the heart of town, Lauretta Elementary, and District 2 Grade School. A new two-story high school was es-

Dawson Central School. Courtesy of Dawson Association.

tablished which eventually employed forty teachers. Class sizes were typically large, with some containing up to 50 students, but behavior problems were minimal because both the parents and children were highly motivated to better themselves. At the time Dawson was closed

Opera House at Dawson.
Courtesy of Dawson Association.

in 1950, it was still the only coal camp in New Mexico with an accredited high school. Through the years, the Dawson schools were also known for their championship sports teams.

The Phelps Dodge Company provided a wealth of recreational activities for its employees. They built a swimming pool, tennis

courts, bowling alley, baseball park, billiard room, movie theater, opera house, and lodge meeting hall. In 1910 the Dawson Opera House was the largest theater in the state, with 800 orchestra-level seats and 200 balcony seats. Traveling vaudeville and stage troupes played at Dawson, and occasionally a circus came to town. In later years motion pictures, featuring major Hollywood stars, were shown in the theater. In 1913 when James Douglas, the Phelps Dodge president, visited Dawson, a fifty-member band greeted him. The band members had no uniforms, so as the president was leaving he asked the general manager to order band uniforms and send the bill directly to him.

As with the schools, Dawson's churches were financed by the company. In 1915 the Protestant church was under the care of Reverend Harvey M. Shields, an Episcopal minister. It was called the "church of

"All Creeds"
Protestant Church.
Courtesy of Dawson Association.

all creeds," but services for several specific denominations were held there. A Catholic priest conducted services in Dawson once every month, but later a large Catholic church was built to meet the growing needs of that denomination.

With all of these advantages, Dawson attracted miners from around the globe. Immigrants came from Italy, Poland, Germany, Great Britain, Greece, Finland, Sweden, Yugoslavia, Mexico, and the Far East to work in the mines at Dawson. The town eventually grew to over 9,000 residents and this small mining area was to supply over a million tons of coal products each year to Arizona, Kansas, Nebraska, New Mexico, Oklahoma, Texas, and many places south of the border in Mexico.

All of the Dawson mines were located on the Blossburg coal seam. The coal beds were oriented horizontally, with only one degree of dip toward the northwest, and this made mining operations less complicated. Ten mines were established in the Dawson area, and they were typically referred to by number. Phelps Dodge made mine safety a high priority, and in 1913 they did such a good job with Stag Canyon Mine No. 2 that engineers and inspectors described it as "the highest achievement in modern equipment and safety appliances that exists in the world." One company publication at that time identified their three most important responsibilities as "first, to the men who work in the mines; second, to the customers; and third, to the stockholders." This approach was certainly revolutionary, even by today's standards.

The primary dangers in coal mining result from the build-up of toxic or explosive gases and coal dust, as well as from the threat of tunnel collapse. Mine inspection reports consistently noted that the Dawson mines were kept free from gas, and this was mainly due to the excellent ventilation systems installed by the company. Large fans were used to circulate up to three times the amount of air required by federal law. The worst mining disasters in history were caused by coal dust explosions, and the management team believed the best way to reduce coal dust was to use water sprayers to prevent dust from mixing with air in the mine. A system of water pipes was run throughout the tunnels, with hose connections ev-

Spraying Water to Reduce Coal Dust.
Courtesy of Dawson Association.

ery 100 feet. Each mine had its own elevated holding tank which guaranteed adequate water pressure using a gravity system. This apparatus also provided a way to suppress any fires that might threaten the mines.

At first, mule-drawn carts and steam-powered trains were used in the mines, but these were rapidly replaced with quieter and safer electric engines. In addition, safety lamps and special explosives were the only ones approved for use in the mines in order to reduce the risk of ignition. A team of fire bosses inspected the tunnels and kept detailed records of mine conditions. Shot firers also inspected each section after blasting and noted any unsafe areas which required attention.

A special tracking system was implemented to check workers in and out of the mines. Each man was given a brass tag stamped with his identification number. A foreman collected the tags when workers entered the mine, and each man called for his tag when he left at the end of his shift. If any tags remained, it was assumed that the man was still in the mine and a search team was dispatched to find him. If he was not found in the mine then the team went to his home, and the search continued until the missing man was found.

Despite these safety measures, Dawson was not immune from mine disasters. On the afternoon of October 22, 1913, an explosion in Stag Canyon Mine No. 2 sent a burst of fire 100 feet out the tunnel entrance and shook buildings in Dawson two miles away. Rescue teams worked around the clock to search for survivors, but only 23 of the 286 workers were found alive. Two rescue workers were also killed, bringing the death toll to 265 men. The small cemetery at Dawson was expanded to accommodate the large number of burials, and white iron crosses marked the graves from this devastating incident.

People of Dawson lined up at the mine entrance after the 1923 explosion.
Courtesy of Raton Museum.

Mine investigators determined that this explosion had been caused by an overcharged blast in a large dusty room. Safety regulations were tightened after the accident, and this helped reduce the severity of future incidents in the Dawson mines. By 1918 these mines reached their peak output of more than four million tons of coal that year.

Tragedy struck again on the afternoon of February 8, 1923. In Stag Canyon Mine No. 1 a coal hauler derailed, damaging the supporting timbers and igniting coal dust in the mine. There were over 120 workers in the mine, and the only survivors were two men working in an isolated area. The Dawson cemetery was again expanded, and new white iron crosses were placed in this area to mark the additional graves. Once again, safety measures were tightened, and the mines continued to operate for almost three decades afterward with only minor incidents.

Market conditions began to change during the first half of the twentieth century. Railroads replaced their coal-burning engines with diesel-electric locomotives. Natural gas and heating oil began to replace coal as a fuel for heating residential and commercial buildings. After World War II many of the mines were closed because of reduced demand, and Stag Canyon Mine No. 6 was the only major producer by 1950.

On April 30, 1950, the Dawson mines were officially closed. This meant that the town of Dawson itself would also be abandoned, and the workers were given thirty days' notice that they must move out of the area. The Phelps Dodge Corporation sold all of the buildings and

Last coal car dumped on April 28, 1950.
Courtesy of Dawson Association.

*Department store
being demolished.*
Courtesy of Dawson
Association.

operating structures to a salvage company, the National Iron & Metal Company of Phoenix, Arizona. The massive coal washing equipment was shipped to Harlan County, Kentucky. Hundreds of small frame cottages were purchased and moved to other locations. Functioning machinery was sold, and everything else was demolished or scrapped and hauled away. This included the department store, bank, opera house, post office, hospital, gymnasium, schools, meeting halls, offices, churches, and scores of other structures that once pulsed with the life of a thriving community. All that remains open to the public today is the Dawson cemetery.

The Phelps Dodge Corporation retained some of the land for a ranching operation called the Diamond D Ranch, and a few of the remaining buildings were occupied by ranch employees. The land began to revert to its natural state and quickly transformed into range land for cattle grazing. Just as it had been in the days when John B. Dawson owned it before 1901, it remains a working ranch to this day.

A Ranch for Boy Scouts

Waite Phillips once wrote that "real philanthropy consists of helping others, outside our own family circle, from whom no thanks is expected or required." He demonstrated this belief by making substantial financial contributions to various charitable organizations and by providing capital funds for building projects undertaken by educational, religious, and welfare institutions.

In 1938 Phillips wrote the President of the Boy Scouts of America, Walter W. Head, with a proposal to donate a portion of the Philmont Ranch to that organization. He believed a successful wilderness camp might be established by the BSA on part of the ranch. In his letter he invited Head and other officials to come to Cimarron to inspect the property he had in mind.

An advance party was dispatched to Philmont by Dr. James E. West, the Chief Scout Executive. These men spent two days horseback primarily in the Ponil country, the area Phillips thought most suitable for a Scout camping operation. They were later joined by West, Head, and Arthur A. Schuck, director of the BSA's Division of Operations. The group discussed at length various ways the property might be developed and used.

Phillips was particularly pleased with the enthusiasm expressed by the group over the proposed site and its potential as a camping area. He especially liked James P. Fitch's assessment that the property represented an opportunity for the BSA to establish a "great university of

From "Scout Camp in the Rockies" by Stephen Zimmer, *Philmont: An Illustrated History*, Irving, Texas: Boy Scouts of America, 1988: 43-64, 125.

the outdoors" unlike anything else in the movement. As he indicated later, Phillips' final decision to make the donation was largely a result of the group's favorable response. He was pleased with the appraisal of the property's recreational value to older members of the Scouting organization.

On October 7, 1938, Phillips wrote President Head to confirm his previous verbal commitment to donate 35,857 acres of the Ponil country together with $50,000 to be used in establishing a camp headquarters. His only stipulation was that the land be used for the benefit of members of the Boy Scouts of America. Phillips suggested that a logical site for a headquarters was Five Points, a spot where the South, Middle, and North Ponil Canyons converged with Horse and Trail Canyons. He felt that trails extending from that point would provide full access to the property, and he suggested the camp be designated a game preserve to allow campers the opportunity to observe the abundant deer, turkey, bear, and other wildlife of the area.

Some discussion had already transpired regarding a suitable name for the camp. Phillips stated that, although a specific name was not a condition of the proposal, he was agreeable to combining part of his name, "Phil," with "turn" indicative of the Scout slogan "Do a good turn daily." He thereby proposed Philturn Boy Scout Park or a similar combination that would serve the organization's needs.

Finally he stated, "If this proposal were being made to any other organization whose rating was inferior to that record of service made by the Boy Scouts of America, I would be inclined to be more particular in outlining a program to be assured that the property would be put to full beneficial use as I visualize it, but I feel amply assured as a result of

Philturn Rockymountain Scoutcamp entrance on Ponil Creek road, about 1939.
Courtesy of Philmont Scout Ranch

your record and in my contacts and conversations with you all, that the executives and advisory board will not accept this property and cash gift unless they feel that it will be beneficial to the Scout programs and that the National Council will provide ways and means for financing its complete development and its operations in the interest of enduring betterment to the youth of America."

Dr. West thereafter issued a statement to the National Executive Board describing the history and physical features of the proposed gift. In part it read, "Each of the canyons is of the same general makeup, flanked on each side by ever changing vistas, rock palisades, timber growth, several highland meadows or mesas, offering excellent additional camping spots. Bear Canyon, Dean Canyon, and Turkey Canyon have an extensive amount of timber growth, comprised principally of western pines, Douglas fir, balsam, quaking aspens and cottonwoods. It is the natural habitat of deer and while on the property we saw mule deer, wild turkeys, and dozens of beaver dams and many evidences of bear."

He further stated that, "while there are few Boy Scout local councils throughout the country which do not have camps both for short camping trips and for summer vacation camping, there is a need of opportunities for troops and patrols with experience, training, leadership and proper equipment to secure the benefits of wilderness camping, which I believe will appeal to older boys in all parts of America. By this is implied a more rugged experience with 'nature in the raw' than is possible in the customary local Boy Scout council camp but at no sacrifice of our essential safeguards of health and safety." His words were to signal the philosophy under which the Phillips ranch properties have operated since the beginning.

The National Executive Board officially accepted the gift on October 20th and in December adopted Philturn Rockymountain Scoutcamp as its name. B.B. Dawson, Scout Executive with councils in Missouri, Kansas, and Nebraska, was the logical choice to develop the new camp. He had broad experience directing various Scout camps, and plans were immediately set in motion to open Philturn in the summer of 1939. Before June three troop camping sites were constructed at Five Points, along with a director's cabin and a commissary building. Cooking shelters and fireplaces were built in Dean Canyon, at Pueblano, and on Stony Point. Burros and saddle horses were purchased and readied for the upcoming camping season.

Scouts at Indian Writings camp, early 1940s.
Courtesy of Philmont Scout Ranch

Equally as important, specific camping policies were created. Because Philturn was considered from the beginning as a laboratory for adventure camping by Senior Scouts, the minimum age requirement was set at fifteen years old. Campers were required to demonstrate, to the satisfaction of local council officials, camping ability and experience adequate to Philturn's wilderness conditions.

Initially, Philturn officials felt that Scouts would derive the greatest benefit from camping on the property if they were encouraged to design their own activities. The headquarters, therefore, was to be a staging and outfitting area from which each group would embark, and each one would provide its own leadership. A group could choose to spend its entire stay backpacking, but it was also possible to take along horses, pack burros, or a Philturn chuckwagon and cook. Scouts could choose a three-day backpack trip or a longer excursion of six or twelve days. These often incorporated side trips to nearby historic and scenic sites like Mount Capulin, the Carson National Forest, Cimarron Canyon, and Taos Pueblo. The weekly rate per camper was set at one dollar, with additional fees for meals, horses, and guide service on longer expeditions. Each group was expected to pro-

Philturn chuckwagon and cook Billy Wetzel.
Courtesy of Philmont Scout Ranch.

vide its own tents and cooking equipment, although tents, blankets, and cowboy sleeping tarps were also available at the headquarters.

A concerted effort was made to publicize the opportunities at Philturn to Scout leaders across the nation and to their boys. Articles appeared in *Scouting* and *Boy's Life* magazines detailing the camp's facilities and programs, emphasizing the wilderness backcountry where so many historic characters once lived. In spite of such promotions, only 189 Scouts from Texas, Kansas, Louisiana, and Oklahoma were able to camp at Philturn that first summer. Nevertheless, construction began in the fall on a headquarters complex at Five Points, including a main lodge to house a kitchen, dining room, and director's office.

By the end of the following season Dawson wrote, "For every Scout or leader who attended during the 1939 season, more than four attended during the season of 1940." National Council Executives were pleased with the response, noting the increase in the number of councils that sent Scouts to Philturn. As was hoped, the camp's program encouraged troops to try adventure camping, and it helped to hold the interest of older boys in Scouting.

The 1941 season opened with the addition of a director's residence and guest house. Also, a building called the 'Longhouse' had been constructed at the mouth of Horse Canyon. It was designed for use by the summer staff, but more importantly it was to serve as a headquarters for Scoutmasters participating in training courses during the spring and fall. The curriculum for these courses would focus on familiarizing leaders with the camp and its program, and to inspire them to bring expeditions of their own in the future. The cost of these buildings and other improvements was $22,000, of which Waite Phillips agreed to pay half.

Phillips was interested in more than facilities at Philturn. He frequently met with Dawson and discussed the camp's operation, sometimes taking the director on horseback rides to point

Buildings under construction at Philturn headquarters.
Courtesy of Philmont Scout Ranch.

1941 map of Philturn Rockymountain Scoutcamp and surrounding area.
Courtesy of Philmont Scout Ranch.

out a particular trail or scenic area that he felt might be included in the program. Phillips often drove to Philturn and sat quietly in his car observing the Scouts in camp. At other times he rode his favorite horse, Gus, among the boys as they made their camps and hiked the trails. Phillips rarely identified himself, but took the opportunity to learn first-hand how they were enjoying themselves. He believed these visits were the best way for him to determine the impact of Philturn on the people he intended to benefit by his gift.

Phillips evidently liked what he saw, for he soon contacted Scout officials about an additional donation much larger than the first. In the fall of 1941 Waite Phillips met with Walter Head, James West, and Arthur Schuck in St. Louis. There he presented a proposal for donating 91,538 acres of mountainous backcountry, his Villa Philmonte home, and the buildings at his Philmont Ranch headquarters. Because he felt that American Scouts and their leaders would benefit from the educational opportunities of a diversified western ranch, he offered to include herds of beef, dairy cattle, sheep, horses, buffalo, hogs, and poultry as part of the gift.

Phillips knew that substantial funds would be necessary for developing a camping operation on the enlarged area. He therefore offered the twenty-three story Philtower building in Tulsa as part of his proposal. The building was then netting $130,000 annually in rental income. The properties were appraised at more than five million dollars. The BSA leaders were astonished at the immensity and generosity of Phillips' offer. They immediately recognized additional possibilities for an expanded camping program on the property, given the many miles of trail and the four mountain lodges Phillips had already built there.

Armed with Phillips' letter of December 11th describing the proposed gifts, President Head gave specifics to the Board and gained unanimous acceptance. It was agreed to consolidate the new ranch property with Philturn and call the unit Philmont Scout Ranch. The decision was announced on December 19th by Phillips in Tulsa. In his statement to the Tulsa *Daily World* Phillips was quoted as saying, "That ranch represents an ideal of my youth...and has meant a lot to my son and his pals. Now I want to make it available to other boys...I'd be selfish to hold it for my individual use."

As with Philturn, Phillips imposed no restrictions on the BSA beyond that the properties be used "for the advancement and development of the program of Scouting." He stated that although he did not "want to make any demand upon the Boy Scouts of America... the ranch has been part of my life for twenty consecutive years. My son grew to manhood there. I would like to reserve for myself and members of my family the right to walk or ride over this property." He further requested that his horse, Gus, be turned out on the ranch, unridden, to live out his life in the fields "white with clover." Those desires were diligently carried out by the managers of Philmont throughout the years.

Although many of Philmont's programs have changed or been added to over the years, the essential elements of a trip to the ranch have not. Today Scouts experience the backcountry much as their predecessors did in the beginning. Aside from having to negotiate rough mountain terrain, the success of each group's trek depends on its members' ability to work together. What campers learn about themselves often proves to be as important as the skills they acquire. Their experience not only fulfills the goals of Scouting, but also meets Waite Phillips' intent in giving the ranch to the BSA.

Phillips himself said it best:

> These properties are donated and dedicated to the Boy Scouts of America for the purpose of perpetuating faith, self-reliance, integrity, and freedom—principles used to build this great country by the American pioneer—so that these future citizens may, through thoughtful adult guidance and by the inspiration of nature, visualize and form a code of living to diligently maintain these high ideals and our proper destiny.
>
> *Waite Phillips, December 1941*

Cimarron Reading List

Armstrong, Ruth. *The Chases of Cimarron*. Albuquerque: New Mexico Stockman, 1981.

Bartholomew, Ed. *Black Jack Ketchum: Last of the Hold-up Kings*. Houston: Frontier Press of Texas, 1955.

Bryan, Howard. *Robbers, Rogues and Ruffians*. Santa Fe: Clear Light Publishers, 1991.

Burton, Jeffrey. *The Deadliest Outlaws: The Ketchum Gang and the Wild Bunch*. Denton: University of North Texas Press, 2006.

Carter, Harvey L. *Dear Old Kit: The Historical Christopher Carson*. Norman: University of Oklahoma Press, 1968.

Caffey, David L. *Frank Springer and New Mexico*. College Station: Texas A&M University Press, 2006.

Cleaveland, Agnes Morley. *Satan's Paradise*. Boston: Houghton Mifflin Company, 1952.

Cleaveland, Norman. *The Morleys: Young Upstarts on the Southwest Frontier*. Albuquerque: Calvin Horn Publisher, 1971.

Fergusson, Harvey. *Grant of Kingdom*. New York: William Morrow and Company, 1950.

Freiberger, Harriet. *Lucien Maxwell: Villain or Visionary*. Santa Fe: Sunstone Press, 1999.

French, William. *Some Recollections of a Western Ranchman: New Mexico, 1883-1899*. New York: Frederick A. Stokes Co., 1928.

—— *Further Recollections of a Western Ranchman*. Ed. Jeff C. Dykes. New York: Argosy-Antiquarian Ltd., 1965.

Guild, Thelma S. and Carter, Harvey L. *Kit Carson: A Pattern for Heroes*. Lincoln: University of Nebraska Press, 1984.

Gunnerson, Dolores A. *The Jicarilla Apaches: A Study in Survival*. DeKalb: Northern Illinois Press, 1974.

Hilton, Tom. *Nevermore, Cimarron, Nevermore*. Forth Worth: Western Heritage Press, 1970.

Keleher, William A. *Maxwell Land Grant: A New Mexico Item*. Santa Fe: The Rydal Press, 1942.

Lambert, Fred. *Bygone Days of the Old West*. Kansas City: Burton Publishing Company, 1948.

Montoya, Maria E. *Translating Property: The Maxwell Land Grant and the Conflict Over Land in the American West, 1840-1900*. Berkeley: University of California Press, 2002.

Murphy, Lawrence R. *Lucien Bonaparte Maxwell: Napoleon of the Southwest*. Norman: University of Oklahoma Press, 1983.

—— *Out in God's Country*. Springer: Springer Publishing Company, 1969.

—— *Philmont: A History of New Mexico's Cimarron Country.* Albuquerque: University of New Mexico Press, 1972.

Parsons, Chuck. *Clay Allison: Portrait of a Shootist.* Pecos, Texas: West of the Pecos Museum, 1983.

Pearson, Jim Berry. *The Maxwell Land Grant.* Norman: University of Oklahoma Press, 1961.

Simmons, Marc. *Kit Carson and His Three Wives.* Albuquerque: University of New Mexico Press, 2003.

Stanley, Francis. *Desperadoes of New Mexico.* Denver: World Press, Inc., 1953.

—— *No Tears For Black Jack Ketchum.* Denver: World Press, Inc., 1958.

—— *The Grant That Maxwell Bought.* Denver: World Press Publishing Company, 1952.

—— *One Half Mile from Heaven or the Cimarron Story.* Denver: World Press Publishing Company, 1949.

Taylor, Morris F. *First Mail West.* Albuquerque: University of New Mexico Press, 1971.

—— *O. P. McMains and the Maxwell Land Grant Conflict.* Tucson: University of Arizona Press, 1979.

Tiller, Veronica E. Velarde. *The Jicarilla Apache Tribe: A History, 1846-1970.* Lincoln: University of Nebraska Press, 1983.

Truett, John A. *Clay Allison: Legend of Cimarron.* Santa Fe: Sunstone Press, 1998.

Wallis, Michael. *Beyond the Hills: The Journey of Waite Phillips.* Oklahoma City: Oklahoma Heritage Association, 1995.

Zimmer, Stephen. *People of the Cimarron Counry.* Parker, Colorado: Eagle Trail Press, 2012.

Zimmer, Stephen and Walker, Larry. *Philmont: An Illustrated History.* Irving, Texas: Boy Scouts of America, 1988.

Also by Stephen Zimmer

People of the Cimarron Country
This book tells the stories of people, both historic and contemporary, who have made the Cimarron country great. Over two dozen biographical sketches, with scores of rare photos that bring these tales to life.   ISBN: 978-0-9851876-4-4

Cowboy Days: Stories of the New Mexico Range
A wonderful collection of stories about working cowboys and their adventures in the ranch country of northeastern New Mexico.   ISBN: 978-0-939549-67-0

Western Animal Heroes: An Anthology of Stories by Ernest Thompson Seton
Naturalist Ernest Thompson Seton wrote spellbinding stories of wild animal courage, intelligence, and endurance in the 1890s.   ISBN: 978-0-86534-356-6

Parker's Colt: A Novel of New Mexico Ranch Life
An authentic portrayal of contemporary ranch life in New Mexico, where horses are still an integral part of working ranches.   ISBN: 978-0-86534-810-3

Philmont: A Brief History of the New Mexico Scout Ranch (with Larry Walker)
This illustrated history tells the story of Philmont primarily with pictures, tracing the ranch's past up through today.   ISBN: 978-0-86534-293-8

Vision, Grace and Generosity (with Nancy Klein)
This lovely volume tells the story of Waite and Genevieve Phillips' philanthropy as they made their generous gift of property and resources to the Boy Scouts of America.

CPSIA information can be obtained
at www.ICGtesting.com
Printed in the USA
FFOW04n1137180417
34615FF